THIS IS *Life*

AND I NEED ANSWERS

Responding to Life's Difficulties

This is Life and I Need Answers

Responding to Life's Difficulties

by Gayla Baughman, Patricia Bollmann, Beverly Burk,
Karla Christian, Evelyn Drury, Melissa Fross, Linda Gleason,
Joy Haney, Phyllis Jones, Mary Loudermilk,
Rebecca Maracich, Priscilla McGruder, Cynthia Miller,
Gwyn Oakes, Linda Poitras, Anne Richardson, Anne Suarez,
Susan Tracy, Barbara Westberg

©2004 Word Aflame® Press
  Hazelwood, MO 63042-2299

Cover Design by Paul Povolni

ISBN 0-75772-912-6

All Scripture quotations in this book are from the King James Version of the
Bible unless otherwise identified.

Printed in United States of America

Printed by

WORD AFLAME® PRESS
8855 DUNN ROAD
HAZELWOOD, MO 63042-2299

contributing writers

Gayla Baughman

Patricia Bollmann

Beverly Burk

Karla Christian

Evelyn Drury

Melissa Fross

Linda Gleason

Joy Haney

Phyllis Jones

Mary Loudermilk

Rebecca Maracich

Priscilla McGruder

Cynthia Miller

Gwyn Oakes

Linda Poitras

Anne Richardson

Anne Suarez

Susan Tracy

Barbara Westberg

contents

foreword

His grace is sufficient! How many times since coming to know the Lord and His wondrous ways have we heard that familiar passage of scripture? How often we have questions that seem to have no answers.

Jesus did not promise that we would be free of the cares of life, but He gave us the promise that He would be with us—even to the end of the age. He has given us the provision of "Casting all your care upon him; for he careth for you" (I Peter 5:7).

There are times, however, when we feel as if we do not understand exactly what to do. In this book, we have endeavored through the Word of God and our own experiences in the same or like situations to answer some of the questions that have come to us from various sources.

The nineteen women who have written the following pages were prayerfully and carefully chosen because we saw faith at work in their lives or because they knew someone who had come through a time of testing or trial.

The authors are all Spirit-filled women and have diligently clung to the Word of God for answers to help you with the critical issues you may be facing now—or will face in the future. If there is a friend who is going through something that is addressed, then use this book as a tool to help her.

In the second chapter of Titus, the older women are instructed to teach the younger, and in verse one we are told to teach the things that become sound doctrine. If we do this, we must always go to the Word of God for answers. This book gives biblical answers for a myriad of questions or problems we face. You will be able to use it as a fundamental teaching tool as well as a personal reference for mentoring the younger women in your life.

It is our prayer that you will be blessed and strengthened as you read the informative, power-packed articles that we have compiled.

Gwyn Oakes
Ladies Ministries President
United Pentecostal Church International

a word
from the editor

In editing this book, I have had the rare privilege of working with a very special and talented group of ladies. Some names you will immediately recognize; others you may not. They come from across the United States and Canada and vary in age from the twenties through middle age. Some are ministers; others, pastors' wives; and others are church members sitting in our congregations. Regardless of their calling in life, each has an important message to share with you.

In the pages that follow, you will look into the hearts of nineteen Spirit-filled ladies and glean from lessons they have learned on how to deal with life's problems through the wisdom of God's Word. Each is uniquely qualified to write what you find here. No names are attached to individual chapters, and this is intentional. Some are writing from personal, and often painful, experience. Others are sharing the stories of those they have counseled through difficult times. It is not the name that matters but the lessons learned.

I cannot tell you to sit back, read, and enjoy. The topics are too crucial. I can tell you to open your heart and take courage. God can—and will—see you through the most difficult situations you ever face. You may find yourself in this book, or you may discover help for a friend.

Whatever the circumstances, let God's Word minister to your needs through the stories of these ladies.

Mary Loudermilk

CHAPTER ONE

Disciplines of a Positive Life

MEETING LIFE WITH A VICTORIOUS ATTITUDE

The negatives of life are very familiar to all of us. Not even those who serve the Lord are immune to the storms and cares of living. Bad things do happen to good people. The danger lies not so much in what may happen to us, but the way those things can shape our attitudes and us.

"In the world ye shall have tribulation" (John 16:33). Tribulation means distress or suffering resulting from oppression or persecution; *also*: a trying experience. Do these words apply in a greater measure to any man more than Job? In a matter of a very short time Job lost his home, his cattle, his servants, and his children. The one remaining constant for Job was his wife and she advised him to "curse God, and die" (Job 2:9). When his friends came to visit, they stared at him for seven days before uttering one word and even then it was to criticize and accuse him. What encouragement was there left for Job?

If any man had a right to feel as though he had been

cheated by life, a right to have a negative attitude and be critical, it was Job. But his reply to all of this was, "What? shall we receive good at the hand of God, and shall we not receive evil?" (Job 2:10). Job realized that life is not fair; it does rain on the just and the unjust. But rather than charge God foolishly, Job said, "Naked came I out of my mother's womb, and naked shall I return thither: the LORD gave, and the LORD hath taken away; blessed be the name of the LORD" (Job 1:21).

Job's attitude was one of faith and confidence in the face of a terrible storm. It was this positive attitude that held Job so that he kept his integrity and in the end not only survived, but also triumphed. Our attitude creates the atmosphere of our lives, governs our reactions, and therefore shapes our destinies. Whether we live a life of victory or defeat is greatly determined by our attitude.

Our Attitude Is Up to Us

There are simple choices at the root of life. And for us, like Job, one of the most basic is the choice of attitude or spirit in which we will live. William James said, "The Greatest Revolution of our generation is the discovery that human beings, by changing the inner attitudes of their minds, can change the outer aspects of their lives."

No attitude is automatic. You are not born with a good attitude or a bad attitude. While tendencies toward optimism or pessimism may be genetic, or influenced by our social environment, in the end we must each day decide our outlook. None need be bitter and broken by life. Our attitude is ultimately a choice.

A positive outlook and mentality are not the result of having only good things to happen, but are the product of an inner life that overcomes the negative by refusing to become negative. Someone said, "Life is 10% what happens to us, and 90% how we react to it." It is true that we cannot control the negative atmosphere of the world around us, but we can choose to control negativism from taking root in our mind and heart. "We cannot choose how many years we will live, but we can choose how much life those years will have" (Anonymous). We may change, grow, and leave one attitude and embrace another. If we recognize in ourselves a tendency toward pessimism, anger, depression, and negativism, we can choose to remain a victim of these in our life or we can change.

Taking Responsibility for Our Attitude

The greatest day in our lives is the day we take total responsibility for our attitude. That is the day we truly grow up! Responsibility means the quality or state of being responsible either morally, legally, or mentally. A negative attitude blames circumstances or people for the difficulties in life rather than accepting the situation and dealing with it personally. If we are grumpy, we say, "I got up on the wrong side of the bed." If failure at something plagues us, we say, "I was born on the wrong side of the tracks." And when nothing seems to be "happening" in our lives, we say, "Everybody else gets the breaks, not me."

A positive attitude recognizes that blaming others has no benefits. Instead, it focuses on the good things that are happening in life. It draws strength from the higher view. This is what the psalmist meant when he said, "I will lift up mine eyes unto the hills, from whence cometh my help. My help cometh from the LORD, which made heaven and earth" (Psalm 121:1-2).

How to Change Our Attitude

Discipline is a means of changing our attitude, but discipline can come only after we have leaned how to harness negative occurrences and actions and turn them into positive situations that cause us to become better, not bitter.

God can show us how to turn our frustrations into fulfillment. Author Richard S. Taylor tells of a professor who found himself marooned in a waiting room one afternoon with no pad to write on or a book to read. Sensing that several hours of important work would be lost, the professor began to tighten up inside. Then deliberately and prayerfully he relaxed and looked around the waiting room. Opposite him was a harried and worried mother with a child in her arms. The little girl was demanding attention and causing an uproar in the waiting room. It was an awkward situation for everyone. With a smile and in a cheerful way, the professor spoke to the child and won her confidence and had the little girl on his lap, where he kept her happily occupied until the very grateful mother was out of the doctor's office and ready to go home. His heart was strangely warmed. The afternoon had not been wasted; it had been invested. This type of story can be told only of those who have disciplined their minds to look for raw material of a negative situation and turn it into a productive, positive situation.

If we discipline ourselves to first fill our minds with "whatsoever things are true, whatsoever things are honest, whatsoever things are just, whatsoever things are pure, whatsoever things are lovely, whatsoever things are of good report" (Philippians 4:8), there will be no room for negative thoughts, criticism, jealousy, or envy. When we have God dwelling in us, we have the power we need to help us discipline our lives, rise above the circumstances, and change our attitudes. Paul reminds us that "I can do all things through Christ which strengtheneth me" (Philippians 4:13).

Discipline in Prayer

One of the areas of discipline we need to cultivate is the area of prayer. I Thessalonians 5:17 admonishes us to "pray without ceasing." There will be days when we will not feel like praying, but those are the days we need to pray the most. Daniel did not wait to be thrown into the lions' den before he prayed. He prayed three times a day even on the good days (Daniel 6:10). When we have disciplined ourselves to daily prayer and adversity does come, we do not have to begin our prayer by saying, "God, remember me? I have not talked to You lately, but I have a problem with which I need help." Rather, we can do as the author of the Book of Hebrews tells us in chapter 4, verse 16: "Let us therefore come boldly unto the throne of grace, that we may obtain mercy, and find grace to help in time of need."

Daily prayer is a necessity for a disciplined person and is one of the eminent characteristics of a positive-minded Christian. If we fortify ourselves with daily prayer, our minds will not be idle to become a workshop for the enemy. This time of prayer is to be focused and not a mere habit or a performance that we go through as a routine. If only a routine, it becomes a dead and ineffective way of prayer. Such prayer will have no changing effect with what we are trying to accomplish—a connection with God that will daily give us strength and courage to become more positive in our spirit and attitude. We may try to excuse our reaction to situations, but the true secret is found in our lack of prayer. Our power with God through prayer is the source of a new attitude of victory.

Discipline in the Word

Our knowledge of the Scriptures can also be extremely beneficial when facing adversity, but we will not have this knowledge if we have not first disciplined ourselves to study the Word of God. We have heard people say, "Pray the scripture when faced with trying situations." This is impossible to do if we have not first

17

committed those scriptures to memory. If there are certain areas of our life that seem to frustrate us more than others, we can find scriptures that relate to that subject and memorize them. You can start out by writing these verses on a card and placing them where they are visible every day. Once you have the verses in your mind, you can quote them on a regular basis so that they are not soon forgotten. The Bible is a source of wisdom and principles that guide us and give us an insight into life that is not available anywhere else.

The Bible, however, is more than just a source of information. It goes far beyond that. There is a transforming effect through the Word of God: "Thy word have I hid in mine heart, that I might not sin against thee" (Psalm 119:11). This illumination does not just come from the principles of the Word, but from the power of God. By hiding the Word in our hearts, we plug into an eternal viewpoint of life that raises the vision from the problems of today and ennobles the Spirit.

Environmental Discipline

To discipline our attitudes includes constructing a wholesome and positive environment. The environment of our lives is made up of the simple things with which we surround ourselves every day—our friends, the books we choose to read, the music to which we listen, the opinions we allow to affect us; even the décor of our homes can affect our spirit or attitude. Dark, dreary, foreboding environments can create a negative, depressing attitude in us. But the opposite is also true: bright, upbeat, affirmative environments brighten our inner lives. When I have a "blue" day, I will make myself a cup of coffee and I will choose to use my daintiest, my most beautiful, all-time favorite cup in the cabinet. I might eat a hot dog, but I am going to get out my good china and use it for my hot dog and chips. Several years ago, when one of my special friends moved to another state, I gave her one of my "special" cups. I told her how it helped me to feel better about any negative or trying situation that I might find myself in. We have laughed together many times at how often we use those cups.

Sometimes we need new friends. Every friend does not respond to a simple gift of a special cup. If we have surrounded ourselves with friends who are negative, fault-finders, criticizers, and gossipers, this type of environment perpetuates itself and becomes a prison where it is always dark, always negative, which no ray of sunshine can penetrate. Some people refuse to be optimistic about their lives; and if we do not have a strong personality, our positive outlook will not have an effect on them.

It is not always necessary, though, to get new friends, but rather we can create new friends out of old friends. We can do this by lifting their attitude and spirit. It is easy to forget that we are a part of their environment. Rather than "dump" our old friends, we become a part of the positive in their lives. There is an old saying: "Rising tides lift all boats." If we can affect our friends' lives in a positive way, then we have caused them to rise to a new dimension in life. By creating a better person within ourselves, we can influence the environment around us and help create better people. It is true that we can throw back into the sea only one star fish at a time, but let us begin with that one.

Each of us has within our hands the ability to change our lives by changing our attitude. We can face the situations of life as a challenge to make us stronger and anchor us as better individuals, or we can allow these same situations to overtake us and make us live in defeat and bitterness. It is ultimately up to us. We can rise above our circumstances because even though Jesus told us that

19

"in the world ye shall have tribulation," He also told us, "be of good cheer; for I have overcome the world" (John 16:33).

CHAPTER TWO

Window Shopping

COMPARING MYSELF WITH OTHERS

"Born to shop."
"Shop until you drop."
"This car stops at all garage sales."

These bumper stickers caricature the American woman's day. We are born shoppers. Surely, the gene is passed to the daughter through the umbilical cord, as the expectant mother with cramped womb and swollen ankles plods up and down the mall. Women are born shoppers.

Window-shopping is a national pastime. We women spend hours oohing and aahing over the expensive items elaborately displayed in the shop windows.

Some women are perfectly content to return from the mall to their ordinary houses, erase visions of what they do not have, and appreciate what they have. These women are blessed with contented hearts.

Others carry these visions home with them, comparing their smudged sofa to the immaculate one in the window at Ethan Allen's. Discontent infects them with greed, resentment, and even anger. It leads to compulsive buying, using plastic cards, piling up an overload of bills.

Still other women have no desire to window shop. Why invite discontentment? Why waste time viewing a living room scene where no one lives and clothes on a fig-ure-perfect model that does not breathe? These women see display windows as dream worlds comprised of dead, inanimate things. For them life is much more than hand-crafted furniture and designer clothes, displayed but never used.

Windows allow us to see two ways. What do I see when I walk pass a shop window? Sometimes I see the shiny trinkets and expensive whatnots that everyone wants but no one needs. Other times I see what is reflected in the window . . . my face and figure. I despise those window reflections. They are like the crazy mirrors at the amusement park. Surely I am not as fluffy as I look in a shop window!

I Look in My Window of Reference

Every woman has a mental display window, a window of reference. As soon as we are able to understand com-parisons, our attention is drawn inward to this window.

"Isn't she cute? She looks just like her Aunt Stacy." Look in the window. Aunt Stacy is on display, set up as a model. Everyone knows that Aunt Stacy is cute, so the child feels pretty good about herself.

"She is so stubborn, not at all like her brother. He is such a good child." Now brother is on display. In the win-dow the child sees a model of perfection, and she sees her image distorted by someone's words. She does not know whether to be mad at her brother or herself, so she har-bors negative feelings about both. If the comparisons continue, the resentment grows.

Girls who are content with who they are, where they are, and what they have do not mentally window shop. They are not affected by the displays of talents, beauty, and riches. Usually these girls have wise parents who have instilled in them a balanced sense of self-worth.

Other girls are born shoppers. They spend hours comparing the visions in their reference windows with the realities in their lives. "If I were talented like Morgan, I'd have more friends." "If my parents weren't so strict, I'd be popular." "If I had clothes like Lindsay's, I'd be happy."

For these girls, the reality never reaches the perfection they envision in the lives of others. They are always grasping for more, borrowing from the future to fulfill today. They grow up to become the compulsive shoppers who max out their credit cards.

"I saw it. I wanted it. I bought it."

Mental window-shopping is a self-centered occupation. It turns our eyes inward. Am I as pretty as she is? Am I as gifted as she is? Am I smarter than she is?

Discontented little girls become anorexic teens and depressed women. When they marry, their spouses and children never quite measure up to the images in their reference windows.

"Chris and Jason just bought a new house in Stonebrook addition, and look at us. We're still living in this dinky little two-bedroom apartment. Aren't you ever going to get that promotion?"

"Why isn't my baby walking? She's almost a year old. My sister's little girl walked when she was nine months old."

"What do you mean? Hold Heidi back in kindergarten? You can't do that. She would be very embarrassed. Her best friend is in the gifted and talented class."

"Ashley had six bridesmaids, so Jocelyn must have at least seven."

An insecure woman thinks about herself constantly. Staring in her reference window, she shrinks emotionally and spiritually. A woman with a balanced sense of self-esteem, confident of her identity in God, moves past the window into the business of life. When she does look in the window, what she sees does not intimidate her. She is in control of the window dressing.

Contrasts Add Appreciation

When a baby is born, the comparisons begin. Or do they start before then? "This baby kicks a lot more than my first one did." From the womb to the grave, comparisons are a fact of life. We cannot escape them, but we can control how they affect us—whether they motivate or intimidate us.

Comparisons are not all bad. How drab life would be if there were no contrasts, if everything, everybody, every day were the same. How could we know joy, if we never felt sorrow? How could we enjoy a sunny day, if clouds never covered the sun? How could we appreciate beauty, if we never witnessed the grotesque?

"God also hath set the one over against the other" (Ecclesiastes 7:14).

Why? To give us a window of reference. If we did not have something to compare life with, we would have no understanding or appreciation of life.

A window can be a blessing or a curse, depending upon what it displays. What is displayed in my window of reference determines my attitude toward life. Or is it the other way around? Does my attitude determine what I display in my window?

I Choose the Display

In childhood we have little or no control over the displays. But, as we mature, we become the window dressers. We assume the power to determine what goes in the window. Our decisions may be influenced by what was displayed in our childhood, but we can change our perspective, if needed.

We place people in our windows . . . family, neighbors, even strangers, and we compare ourselves with them. The problem surfaces when we dress our windows with the wrong images. Some women have better figures, nicer homes, and more money to spend than we do; some have all the answers. Others have more flab, shabbier homes, less money, and neither the questions nor the answers. Some know God better than we do and others do not know Him at all.

If we place someone who is less blessed than we are in our reference windows, we grow arrogant. If we put someone there who is more fortunate, we become envious. Window-shopping can turn us into bipolar emotional messes.

I listened enthralled as a gifted, anointed speaker told about coming upon an accident scene. She told how she prayed for the injured person; in Jesus' name she commanded the flow of blood to stop. She went to the hospital, witnessed to the family, and won several to the Lord.

Immediately, I decided, "I'm going to be just like her. If I ever come upon an accident, I'm going to do that."

Then one day I had my chance. The car in front of me made a left turn right into the path of a motorcycle. The couple on the cycle went flying through the air. The man landed face down on the highway; the woman landed on her feet running and screaming.

I rolled down my window and shouted, "I'm going to call for help!" I raced to the nearest phone. After reporting the accident, I stood there trembling until the ambulance came; then I returned to the scene.

Weeks later I remembered, "I was going to be like that speaker, but I didn't even think to pray!"

In a moment of crisis, my true self was revealed. I am not a spiritual giant. I am myself, complete with fears and flaws. When I put that gifted, anointed lady in my window of reference, I came up, oh, so short.

Having a role model is fine. But remember, that person is a "model," not a mold.

To say that Jesus is my role model and I strive to be like Him sounds good. It is ideal. But I am human and my motives are not always ideal. My eyes are not always fixed on Jesus Christ. (Sorry! But it is true.) In my window I see people and I see myself—and I struggle with my humanity.

So what do I display in my window of reference? Paul gave us the answer in his letter to the church at Rome.

"For I say, through the grace given unto me, to every man that is among you, not to think of himself more highly than he ought to think; but to think soberly, according as God hath dealt to every man the measure of faith. For as we have many members in one body, and all members have not the same office: so we, being many, are one body in Christ, and every one members one of another. Having then gifts differing according to the grace that is given to us" (Romans 12:3-6).

The Message translation says it in everyday English. "The only accurate way to understand ourselves is by what God is and by what he does for us, not by what we are and what we do for him.

"In this way we are like the various parts of a human body. Each part gets its meaning from the body as a whole, not the other way around. The body we're talking about is Christ's body of chosen people. Each of us finds our meaning and function as a part of his body. But as a chopped-off finger or cut-off toe we wouldn't amount to much, would we? So since we find ourselves fashioned into all these excellently formed and marvelously functioning parts in Christ's body, let's just go ahead and be what we were made to be, without enviously or pridefully comparing ourselves with each other, or trying to be something we aren't.

The Church Becomes My Reference Window

To live a balanced life and walk in contentment while striving for perfection, I put "Christ's body of chosen people," the church, in my reference window. I remind myself that my purpose comes from my function in the body. I do not give the body meaning; the body gives me meaning.

When I view myself not in competition with others, but as a member functioning within the body, I am content to be what I was made to be.

I may not sing like Sister Esther, but I can decorate the foyer. I may not wear designer clothes like the sister on the pew behind me, but I can wear a smile that draws visitors back to our church. I may not have a perfect figure or brilliant children or a rich husband, but I have the mind of Christ. I am a vital part of this body, using the gifts God has given me.

We stand in awe at the creativity of God in nature. No two snowflakes alike; no two thumbprints alike. Awesome! Yet, we struggle against the creativity of God in our lives. Why am I so different from my siblings, my peers, everyone else? Because I am part of God's incredible plan—each one unique.

The next time you look in your window of reference and see something that makes you feel envious or proud, change the display. You are in charge of the window dressing. Dress it to spotlight the church, the body of Christ. It is a grand display sure to bring glory to God and contentment to your soul.

CHAPTER THREE

The Balanced Life

DEALING WITH EVERYDAY STRESS

*W*omen must take time and turn aside out of their busyness to set their priorities in order, for life is a gift and should be lived well!

We all have emergencies where we burn the candle at both ends, but this should not be the norm or soon there will be no candle left to burn. That candle is the spirit within us that inspires us and propels us into forward motion. Psalm 18:28 helps us understand where that inspiration comes from: "For thou wilt light my candle: the LORD my God will enlighten my darkness." The darkness refers to our confusion, hesitation, frustration, or anything that would put out the light within us, as life has been known to do.

James Burns wrote the following story that depicts a good balance: "A famous historic symbol to express moderation is the device of a dolphin twisted round an anchor. This was inscribed on his coins by Titus, the Emperor of

Rome, and was meant to him to express that golden means between hurry and delay—the failure which comes from rushing without premeditation, and hesitation through overmuch caution. The anchor is thus the symbol of delay, and also of firmness and security, while the dolphin is regarded as the swiftest and most mercurial of fish.

"Frequently the dolphin and anchor are used as a family crest, with the motto, *Festina lente*, 'Hasten slowly.' The symbol, fitly expresses the idea of moderation, of that just balance between two opposing forces. It represents maturity in business, which is the medium between too great haste and too great hesitation."

Caught Between Two Forces

Moderation here is described as *that just balance between two opposing forces*. The truth about life is that it is a war. Every day we fight. The newborn baby comes out of the birth canal fighting and gasping for air. She has begun the fight of life. She will fight for the things that are worthwhile. There will be a constant fight between good and evil. Life will hand her situations that will cause her to fight for her very life and for the life of her family.

Finding balance in life—that balance between the two opposing forces, the one that will make her better or the one that will make her bitter—applies to all age groups, as the principles remain the same. It is essential to keep the most important things on the top of the list and to allow proper time for these things so that one does not burn out, become frazzled or haggard.

As we examine the subject more closely we learn that balance means to be poised, have stability, and a steadiness. Related words are *moderation* and *temperate*. Moderation is to be reasonable, sensible, judicious, and temperate.

Philippians 4:5 commands us: "Let your moderation be known unto all men. The Lord is at hand."

Since *moderation* is so closely associated with the word *temperate*, what does it mean to be temperate? The following words describe temperate: pleasant (not angry), calm (not upset), self-controlled (governing our appetites, time, thoughts, etc.), controlled (not out of control), peaceable (living within the boundaries of God's laws), and composed (not frantic).

In I Corinthians 9:25, Paul compares the subject of temperance to a race: "And every man [woman] that striveth for the mastery is temperate in all things. Now they do it to obtain a corruptible crown; but we an incorruptible."

Verses 26 and 27 go on to speak of the discipline required: "I therefore so run, not as uncertainly; so fight I, not as one that beateth the air: but I keep under my body, and bring it into subjection."

Paul knew where he was going: he was disciplined, and walked each day with his priorities in proper order. Women must take time out of their busyness to set their priorities in order as well. We need not beat the air, but walk purposely toward goals, living each day as if it were our last day on earth. We must give our best to each moment that is given to us by God; for life is a gift and should be lived well!

Temperance is one of the fruits of the Spirit mentioned in Galatians 5:22-23. Fruit means there is growth. We may not have it right now, but we can *grow* it in Jesus' name. We *can* become that person we desire to be. We can be the one that has it all together, that has order in her life and has a wonderful relationship with Jesus Christ and with all the people who are in her life, as well as feeling fulfilled in her own personal life.

The Process of Addition

The apostle Peter gives instructions as to what we need to do to help us in this endeavor. He says it is a *process of addition.* He begins in II Peter 1:5: "And beside this, giving all diligence, add to your faith virtue; and to virtue knowledge."

He continues on to name the things that we should add: to knowledge add *temperance*; to temperance, *patience*; to patience, *godliness*; to godliness, *brotherly kindness*; to brotherly kindness, *charity.* He sums it up with this promise in II Peter 1:10: "Wherefore the rather, brethren, give diligence to make your calling and election sure: for if ye do these things, ye shall never fall."

This scripture indicates that we did not initially have these things, but we are going to add to what we do have—which is *faith*.

The word *moderation* also lists *judicious* as a related word. What does it mean to be judicious? A woman who is judicious makes plans that are well thought out; she is thoughtful, sensible, and prudent.

To be *prudent* means to be careful, sensible, practical, discreet, wise, and farsighted. Proverbs 19:14 states that "a prudent wife is from the LORD." Wisdom and prudence are friends and are linked together as they are described in Proverbs 8:12: "I wisdom dwell with prudence." These two attributes were found in Jesus as Paul wrote in Ephesians 1:8: "Wherein he hath abounded toward us in all wisdom and prudence."

Proverbs 31:26 portrays the virtuous woman as being a wise woman: "She openeth her mouth with wisdom." To be prudent, temperate or balanced means to be wise.

Planning Well and Executing the Plan

Finding balance is about finding order, planning well and then executing the plan. And, yes, even handling emergencies that occur frequently. A balanced woman has a plan and knows where she is going. She does not just beat the air but works faithfully each day at keeping her priorities at the top of her life. The priorities should include God being first, and then prioritizing family, time for self, others, responsibilities, jobs, etc. She plans her work; then she works her plan.

When Carl J. Printz, the Commissioner from Sweden to Canada for many years, turned ninety-nine years old, he was asked for rules by which such a long and useful life might be achieved. He replied: "I would suggest one definite rule and that is, one must be temperate in all things." Then he added quickly: "Perhaps I should say all but one, for in the Bible you can read the commandments to love the Lord with all your heart, soul and mind, and your neighbor as yourself. These are the only things we can rightly do to excess."

Time for God

My strong belief is that a constant relationship with Jesus Christ is essential for a woman to be balanced, to have purpose, to have faith, to overcome trials, to be a good wife, mother, and friend, and all the other things that are expected of her.

Jesus said to seek God first: "But seek ye first the kingdom of God, and his righteousness; and all these things shall be added unto you" (Matthew 6:33).

This should be our *first* priority. It colors everything else we do. Find time each day to spend moments in prayer with the One who calms spirits, who heals broken hearts, who gives inspiration, direction, and strength for the tasks that await you.

During this time of prayer have a notebook and pen with you, and as things come to your mind write them down. By writing them down you will not forget them, and then you can deal with them *after* prayer. Bits of inspiration will come to you as you pray, so write them down also. If God speaks clearly to you concerning a situation, then write it down. Do not be concerned about legibility or neatness; just write it down. You can organize your thoughts later. This practice will alleviate distractions, and you will be able to keep your mind focused on prayer.

This is important for Isaiah 26:3 declares: "Thou wilt keep him in perfect peace, whose mind is stayed on thee: because he trusteth in thee."

Time for Family

Titus 2:4-5 tells us what the older women are supposed to teach the younger women: "That they may teach the young women to be sober, to love their husbands, to love their children. To be discreet, chaste, keepers at home, good, obedient to their own husbands, that the word of God be not blasphemed."

The central subject of Paul's discourse is the family. The family is most important. As I have said to the young women, "Your children are your first congregation. You need to teach them about God, how to live and love, and bring them to salvation."

Not only will it lead them to salvation but also it will help to take care of their needs emotionally and physically, and teach them how to mature properly and become fulfilled. A family is a big responsibility and should be looked upon not only as a duty but also as a privilege that God has placed in your hands.

The following paragraph issues a challenge of what one man asked women to be willing to do:

> "Are you willing to stoop down and consider the needs and the desires of little children; to remember the weakness and loneliness of people who are growing old; to stop asking how much your friends love you, and ask yourself whether you love them enough; to bear in mind the things

that those who live in the same house with you really want, without waiting for them to tell you; to trim your lamp so that it will give more light and less smoke, and to carry it in front so that your shadow will fall behind you; to make a grave for your ugly thoughts, and a garden for your kindly feelings, with the gate open?"

—HENRY VAN DYKE [1]

Time for Self

Arnold Bennett worked as a poverty-stricken young clerk in a London law office until the day he wrote his best-selling book, *How to Live on Twenty-Four Hours a Day*. The book was a success because everyone thought they did not have enough time in one day to do the things that needed done. He had somehow captured the nugget of truth that we all have as much time as we will ever have. It is how we manage our time that is important.

He wrote: "Time is the inexplicable raw material of everything. With it, all is possible; without it, nothing. You wake up in the morning, and lo! Your purse is magically filled with twenty-four hours of the unmanufactured tissue of the universe of your life! It is yours. It is the most precious of possessions . . . No one can take it from you. It is unstealable. And no one receives either more or less than you receive. You have to live on these twenty-four hours of daily time. Out of it, you have to spin health, pleasure, money, contentment, respect, and the evolution of your immortal soul. Its right use, its most effective use, is a matter of the highest urgency and of the most thrilling actuality. Your happiness—the elusive prize that you are all clutching for, my friends—depends on that."

There it is in a nutshell: we all have the same amount of time. It is how we spend our time that makes the difference. We need to be good managers of our time. It is important for each of us to have some time alone doing something enjoyable, or to take time and spend it in having fun with others. This fun time feeds our soul and spirit and makes us better women. It enables us to have a calm spirit in our dealings with others.

Handling Stress

Stress is a part of each of our lives. It is very real. Prolonged stress accompanied with tension will eventually show on our face. It is inside us and announces to others that we are "under stress," as it is often labeled.

Stress has a familiar pattern: worry, strain, and nervous tension accompanied with a frenzy of rush and hurry. It is a feeling of having too much to do, too many problems, feeling driven and distraught. Stress causes women to become mentally and emotionally upset. They are out of balance!

Handling stress is basically finding balance in our life. Jesus gave the secret two thousand years ago in Matthew 6:25-26: "Take no thought for your life, what ye shall eat, or what ye shall drink; nor yet for your body, what ye shall put on. . . . Behold the fowls of the air: for they sow not, neither do they reap, nor gather into barns; yet your heavenly Father feedeth them. Are ye not much better than they?"

He is basically saying, "Don't worry or be full of anxiety. Relax! Let God help you with the unknown and with the cares of life. He will take care of you!"

Years ago in addressing a group of students at Yale, Sir William Osler, penned the following words: "The load of tomorrow, added to that of yesterday, carried today makes the strongest falter . . . Waste of energy, mental distress and nervous worries dog the steps of a man [woman] who is anxious about the future."

If we can only realize that life comes to us in moments, one moment at a time, and that if we can relax for one moment, then another, we can gain hours of living without anxiety and tension. It may be necessary to tell yourself, "Relax! Jesus is helping me and giving me peace in this situation. He will work all things out for my good."

Learn to sing, hum, or whistle while you work, or surround yourself with some inspirational music. Make yourself smile instead of frown. Laugh instead of worry. Throw back your head and laugh a good belly laugh, even if you do not feel like it. Your body will respond. Proverbs 17:22 declares it to be so: "A merry heart doeth good like a medicine: but a broken spirit drieth the bones."

The *Contra Costa Times* printed an article entitled "Prayer" in the Sunday, January 21, 1996, issue which stated:

"'People assume thoughts are free: that as long as you only think things, it is no big deal,' said James Billings, senior vice president of the Sausalito institute. 'Now we know if we think it, our body experiences it. Stress, worry, fear—all of that has an effect on our physiology.' . . . 'Faith in general is good for your health,' said Dr. Dale Matthews, an internist at Georgetown University Hospital in Washington, D.C. 'Faith is in the same category as eating a low-cholesterol diet and exercising regularly.'"

There it is again: relax! Have faith in God to help you, to be with you, and to work all things out. The Word of God helps one to relax. It is inspirational, soothing, and helps cut out the thoughts that are debilitating to your system. "For the word of God is quick, and powerful, and sharper than any twoedged sword, piercing even to the dividing asunder of soul and spirit, and of the joints and marrow, and is a discerner of the thoughts and intents of the heart" (Hebrews 4:12).

This is why it is an absolute necessity that in order to maintain good emotional balance we must put God and His Word on our daily calendar. Do not pencil Him in, write it with indelible ink. Women who leave God out welcome stress in—and become stressed out.

Take time to pray in a quiet place, read the Scriptures in a quiet place, and learn to soar as promised in Isaiah 40:31: "But they that wait upon the LORD shall renew their strength; they shall mount up with wings as eagles; they shall run, and not be weary; and they shall walk, and not faint."

Learning to Say No

Joseph Addison once wrote, "The grand essentials to happiness in this life are something to do, something to love, and something to hope for." This is true as long as the *something to do* does not turn out to be bigger than everything else. If the *something to do* overshadows all else in life, then life gets out of proportion and women lose the rhythm or balance of a contented life.

People can be demanding of you, schedules can become jammed, tension can be the norm, and everything can get out of whack when you take on too much to do with too little time to do it. This particular subject is written to the women who are known as *givers*. They give and give, even when their strength is depleted and they feel drained. They allow others to fill up their calendar and never learn to say no. They just keep saying, "Yes, I'll do it," all the while their spirit is crying out for some rest or a break from the demands others place upon them.

There are times when a busy woman needs to stop and contemplate, to sit quietly somewhere, perhaps on a porch, in a wooded glen, by a rippling brook, at the edge of the ocean, or even in a secluded park. Years ago I read the story of some Americans who were exploring Africa and had hired native guides. Each day they pushed the guides to go faster and a little bit farther, until one day the guides sat down and refused to go. The Americans could not understand them and asked, "Why do you sit down when we have so far to go?" The guides replied, "We are letting our soul catch up with our body."

A woman can become so involved that instead of stopping and resting or doing something that takes their mind completely off the thing that spurs her on, she just keeps pushing to get as much done in as little time possible.

How does one say *no*? It is very simple. Just say no! There are several ways to do this. If you are fatigued from doing too much and the joy you once knew is gone, your family may be getting the leftovers of your life. If you need a break, the following phrases might give you an idea of how to say no:

"I'm sorry, but my schedule will not allow it. I regret that I have to say *no*, but thank you for asking me."

"This is not going to work for me. I've over-scheduled and regretfully I'm going to have to say no at this time. So sorry!"

Choose this day to seek God first, and He will help you as you listen quietly to the great plans He has for your life. He will teach you how to balance all things well!

---

[1] Howell, Clinton T, edited by, *Lines to Live By*, (THOMAS NELSON INC.: New York, NY: 1972), p. 130.

CHAPTER FOUR

Do Dreams Really Come True?

HOW TO OVERCOME LIFE'S DISAPPOINTMENTS

The future held great promise as she married and then had two wonderful sons. Filled with dreams and aspirations for this young family of hers, she envisioned many things for their future. All was well for several years as life moved in predictable paths. Then came the disappointments. As the economy grew worse in their town, her husband decided that they must move somewhere which offered a better chance of meeting their needs.

The new place was not like home—the people were different, their customs were different, and even their religion was different. The family knew no one there, but, as one does, they adjusted. Soon things did not seem quite as strange as they settled into their new routine.

By the time the boys were ready to marry and have their own families, the differences did not seem to matter as much anymore. Oh, she would have liked daughters-in-law from back home, but these were nice young women and she grew to love them. Life was not perfect, but it was still good.

But then trouble came again to her doorstep. First her husband died, and then unexpectedly both of her sons died. The life that began with many hopes and dreams now stretched before her empty. One by one, the things she loved had been taken away. Her dreams lie in shattered pieces.

Alone except for one devoted daughter-in-law, she gathered her few possessions and returned to her old home—empty. Why dream more dreams? She had no hope that her dreams would be fulfilled. Even her name, bestowed at birth with so much promise, now served as a reminder of all she no longer possessed. "Call me not Naomi [pleasant], call me Mara [bitter]: for the Almighty hath dealt very bitterly with me. I went out full, and the LORD hath brought me home again empty" (Ruth 1:20-21).

Life Can Be Disappointing

Have you ever felt that life did not fulfill all your hopes and dreams? Is there an emptiness inside that you cannot explain to others? On the surface your life may appear pleasant, and even your best friend may not realize the disappointment you feel at the hopes and longings that have never come to pass.

All of us have unfulfilled desires which we have not seen become reality. No two situations are alike. The things I struggle with and hope for may not affect you at all. And if I were to see your unspoken longings, I might wonder why such an insignificant thing would even ripple the waters of your life. We might look at each other and think, "Oh, she really has it all together," while inside we feel distressed, disappointed, or even cheated. Solomon said that "hope deferred maketh the heart sick" (Proverbs 13:12).

At other times, it is the sudden, unexpected event that

disrupts our plans and dreams. "People can never predict when hard times might come. Like fish in a net or birds in a snare, people are often caught by sudden tragedy" (Ecclesiastes 9:12, NLT). For you, this might mean a serious financial setback, the death of a spouse, personal illness, or other event that leaves you feeling helpless.

Like Job, you may mourn the life that has been swept away in a whirlwind of tragedy.

Like Hannah, you may suffer the pain of infertility.

Like David, you may see your plans put on hold and left to the next generation to build your temple.

Like Jeremiah, you may be asked by God to serve Him in singleness.

Like Paul, you may desire to reach new places for the gospel but find yourself in a "prison situation" where you cannot fulfill your ambitions for your ministry.

Like Joseph and Daniel, you may find yourself far from home and in a situation not of your choosing.

How do you deal with life when it is not all you had hoped? How do you cope? How do you hold on to your dreams when they seem distant or impossible?

There are three things that we must consider about dreams:

- ❀ Not all dreams will be fulfilled, but God may have a plan that will far exceed what you determined for yourself—if you are only willing to trust Him.
- ❀ Sometimes our dreams are deferred and fulfillment will come through another.
- ❀ Sometimes our dreams are unfulfilled because we have unrealistic expectations.

Trust God and Allow Him to Work

Solomon tells us that "people cannot see the whole scope of God's work from beginning to end" (Ecclesiastes 3:11, NLT). God is orchestrating events and outcomes that are hidden by our limited natural sight. Remind your-self often that God is at work behind the scenes.

We must remember that God is "the author and fin-isher of our faith" (Hebrews 12:2). That means that He is the one who begins the good work in us. If He is the author, or the beginning of our faith in hopes and dreams, then He is working all along to finish those things He has begun in us. If He is the finisher, then He is in charge of what happens to us as long as we stay in His will.

We do not know all that it may actually take for our dreams to become reality. The delay in their fulfillment may be God's way of testing us to see how much He can trust us. We may be going through a refining process. Trials are often what shapes our character and helps us to become more like Christ—the ultimate goal, dream, or desire in the heart of a Christian.

Charles Spurgeon wrote: "Happy is the man who hath one desire, if that one desire is on Christ. If Jesus be a soul's desire, it is a blessed sign of divine work within." The Lord has plans for our lives (Jeremiah 29:11), but He also directs us in Psalm 37:4-5 to "delight thyself also in the LORD: and he shall give thee the desires of thine heart. Commit thy way unto the LORD; trust also in him; and he shall bring it to pass."

As we seek ways to achieve our dreams, it is impor-tant that we increase our prayer life. Prayer combined with study of the Word will help our minds stay focused on the spiritual and not be diverted from the right path. God is a rewarder of those that diligently seek first the kingdom of God and His righteousness (Matthew 6:33 and Hebrews 11:6).

God May Have a Different Plan

There is an old saying: "What you are will live on in someone else." Although our dreams may never come to pass in our lifetime, if we plant the seeds of our dream in the heart of another, it will live on. Perhaps the timing is not right for our dreams to be fulfilled, or perhaps God intends it to live on in someone else. That was the case with King David. Although he had a strong desire to build a house for the Lord, God did not allow him to fulfill that dream. Instead God permitted Solomon, his son, to be the instrument of the dream's fulfillment. David accepted God's will and poured his energies into doing all he could to see that dream come to pass through Solomon (I Chronicles 22).

While David knew that his dream would be completed through his son, it is doubtful that Naomi had any such assurance. Although her life did not end on the bitter note of Ruth 1:21 when she declared herself empty, she most likely never realized what hope lie in her arms as she nestled Ruth and Boaz's son, Obed, to her. She felt a certain joy and contentment at holding this promise of the future, but little did she know that the child in her arms would be the grandfather of a king and in the lineage of the King of kings. God did not reveal His ultimate plan to her, even though He was working through her all the time.

God's Word tells us that "to every thing there is a season, and a time to every purpose under the heaven" (Ecclesiastes 3:1). Perhaps, like David, He will reveal that time to us; we may be like Naomi who held the promise of the future but did not realize the full scope of what was within her hands. We speak of Ruth and her dedication, yet we should not forget the life of the mother-in-law who inspired Ruth to leave behind the gods of her people and follow the one true God. God in His time fulfilled the dream in a way Naomi could never imagine or live long enough to see.

I May Be Dreaming the Wrong Dream

We must be careful to dream the right dreams. God's plan for us is perfect, and it is important that we ask Him to make us sensitive to His direction and purpose for our lives. He will show us if our dreams are in His will.

Our desires and dreams ultimately determine how we live. That is why the child of God must have godly desires. Proverbs 4:23 admonishes us to "keep thy heart with all diligence; for out of it are the issues of life." Some dreams can take us in the wrong direction and our spiritual life will suffer because of it. If we pursue the wrong desires, God may not always put a roadblock in our way. Psalm 106:15 tells us, "And he gave them their request; but sent leanness into their soul." That is why we must align ourselves with what God wants for us and set boundaries on our desires.

It may be that we desire good things but that our goals are too lofty or we are personally unable to achieve them. If that be the case, we must evaluate ourselves to see whether we are qualified to attain that dream. It may be helpful to take time to evaluate our personal strengths and weaknesses. We can ask questions such as:

❀ What types of things do I really enjoy?

❀ What do I think are my God-given abilities?

❀ What things create strong feelings or emotions within me?

❀ What people can I surround myself with who are capable of helping me see the dream happen?

Recently a friend worried aloud about conditions in the world and expressed hopelessness that one person could make a difference. Her focus was too broad—changing the whole world—so she set herself up for disappointment. It is true that you or I may not be able to alter the whole picture, but we can make a difference in our part of the picture. I encouraged this friend to consider instead how she could be a positive influence within her community, within her circle of friends, within her immediate world. From that perspective, each of us can make a difference, and the ripple effect from our actions will reach far beyond what we imagined. Perhaps we would do well to look at what is within our reach and then let God expand our circle of influence. Our dream can grow as we prove ourselves faithful first with what is at hand.

Do you long to go to the far reaches of the earth to win the lost? First show yourself faithful in winning your neighbor. God will expand your area of influence and open up more opportunities as you prove yourself faithful where you are.

Do you aspire to be a great speaker and move large crowds with the eloquence of your words? First dedicate yourself to teaching or speaking in your local congregation. If you never make it to the "big time," a life you touch there may go on to be the world-changer you desired to be.

Do you dream of finding that top job with a fantastic salary? Show yourself to be a conscientious employee where you are that others may see your potential for advancement.

Did you forfeit dreams of a career when you married and had children? Do you long to develop your art ability, musical talent, or teaching skills? (You know what to fill in here.) Yes, you can fulfill your family responsibilities and still set apart time to devote yourself to that talent or ability you wish to develop. It may be only an hour each week now, but you will keep your dream alive for the future. Determine today to take one small step back toward your dream. So what if you never become a concert pianist! You will still have created beautiful music for yourself now. Live in the present as you work toward the future.

Perhaps you dreamed of having many of the good things in life and then unforeseen events took them away. Do you feel like Job who lost it all in just a short span of time? Perhaps it was an illness, the sudden death of your spouse, or a divorce that interrupted your dreams. Then you must alter your dream to create a *good life* even if you cannot have all the *good things*. Things do not bring happiness (Ecclesiastes 2:11 and 5:10). Your children will remember the happiness of your home long after the disappointment of not owning the latest electronic gadget has faded.

Have you ever gone on a journey and been so focused on reaching your destination that you missed all the scenery along the way? Life can be like that. We can become so caught up in our desires that we forget to enjoy the journey. We allow what we do not have to steal the joy of what we do possess. Do not be afraid to dream—one must dream—but until you reach that highest desire, do not neglect that which is within your grasp right now.

Dreaming Is Not Enough

Dreams are only dreams unless we work to fulfill them. We may have to get dirt under our fingernails—struggle and push—to see our dreams materialize. They will not come without effort. II Timothy 2:15 says to "study to shew thyself approved unto God." Fulfilled dreams come with determination, effort, and, yes, even sacrifice. How hard are we willing to work to accomplish that dream?

The writer of Proverbs knew the importance of aspirations or goals (Proverbs 21:5). Without goals we are at the mercy of those strong figures around us. If we do not give serious thought to our goals, how can we realize our dreams? Studies show that people who set goals concentrate better, are more satisfied with their lives, and have less anxiety.

Keeping our goals short and achievable will help us to see ourselves making progress. Webster defines a goal as:

"an object or end that one strives to attain; aim." Dream is defined as "a fond hope or aspiration." One can hardly be separated from the other. It is to our advantage to set short-term as well as long-term goals, and in so doing we will actually see our dreams begin to come to pass. The journey will be much more enjoyable if we actually see the signs of a measure of success occasionally.

Disappointments? Or God's Appointments?

Christians respond to life's disappointments in different ways.

- ❀ Some become angry at God, whining and complaining that He is unfair in letting this illness, handicap, job loss, broken relationship, depression, financial loss (fill in the blank) happen to them.
- ❀ Some assume a martyr complex, letting everyone around them know just how much they are suffering. Their lives lack joy because they expect to be miserable.
- ❀ The wise Christian rejoices and gives thanks in all circumstances of life (Philippians 4:4; I Thessalonians 5:16, 18), allowing God's power to compensate for their weakness.

Elizabeth Elliot once said, "If God, like a father, denies us what we want now, it is in order to give us some far better thing later on. The will of God, we can rest assured, is invariably a better thing."

When we feel disappointed, perhaps even cheated, out of the things we desired for our lives, is it possible that these are really appointments with God that will bring us to a better place? "For the LORD God is a sun and shield: the LORD will give grace and glory: no good thing will he withhold from them that walk uprightly" (Psalm 84:11). This verse assures us that God is our protector.

He gives grace! He gives glory! He does not withhold the good things from us.

Yes, we may have adversity (John 16:33). Yes, there will be setbacks in life. Yes, we may experience disappointments. But God is using those difficulties to shape us into His image (Romans 8:29).

What greater dream can we possess than to be like Him!

CHAPTER FIVE

Money Matters

HOW TO DEAL WITH DEBT

You would be a rare individual indeed if you have not made some unwise choices at some point in your life. Could it be that one of these unwise decisions was about a financial judgment? If you are battling through life with difficulties due to wrong money management, there is hope.

A recent poll in a Christian magazine stated that the number one thing couples argue about most is money and their partner's spending habits.

All of us at some time or another have been in debt more deeply than we would like. It is also quite possible that a major life event—a job loss, death, illness, or divorce—was the cause more than just bad spending habits. Whatever the reason, nobody likes the dreaded D-word (debt), and all want to be free of it. While it probably is not possible to be one hundred percent debt-free, we can learn to manage the debt we have.

The first thing that people in financial trouble think is that they cannot afford to pay tithes on their income to the church. Making the decision not to pay tithes is a major step in the wrong direction. When we do not allow the Lord to help us in our financial matters, we rob not only God but also ourselves.

There is not one of us who has an option on whether we give or do not give ten percent of our income to God. "Will a man rob God? Yet ye have robbed me. But ye say, Wherein have we robbed thee? In tithes and offerings" (Malachi 3:8). We would not consider doing anything illegal to obtain money to pay our bills, but that is what we are doing when we do not give God what is His. God loves you and wants to supply your needs; give Him a chance to do a miracle for you. Matthew 6:33 says, "But seek ye first the kingdom of God, and his righteousness; and all these things shall be added unto you." If you want God to supply your needs, He must come first. Tithing and giving offerings are for our benefit, and God is bound by His promises.

Debt starts early for many. It is not unusual for young people to get their first credit cards when heading off to college—or even before. They then begin to add purchase after purchase to their cards for textbooks, tuition, clothes, and even electronic equipment. Soon, young cardholders are calling up Mom and Dad to bail them out. Nobody has told them that they will have a wrecked credit rating on their future attempts to borrow for a car or a house.

Do you suspect that you have gone too far into debt? If you ask yourself the question, "Am I in trouble?" then you probably are. Are you afraid to open up bills? Can you afford only minimum payments? Or do you wait to the last minute to pay your bills? If so, you need to look at the following steps to getting out of debt.

❀ *Stop going further into debt.*

Romans 13:8 advises us to "owe no man any thing, but to love one another." Financial advisors often recommend that you destroy your credit cards; however, credit cards are not always your biggest problem. You must also watch other sources of debt such as car loans and mortgages. It is easy to get caught up in the excitement of buying a new car or house and then find yourself signing on for more debt than you anticipated. It takes real discipline not to be pressured or enticed to something "bigger and better."

❀ *Track your cash.*

Watch everything that you spend, not just credit-card purchases. Simply writing down every purchase—cash included—can help you see where your money is going. If you have access to a computer, use a software program to chart your spending habits (e.g. *Quicken* or *Microsoft Money*). Keep totals on a daily, weekly, and monthly basis. (Otherwise, you can achieve the same results with a small notebook and pen in your purse.) Faithfully doing this for several months will give you a good idea of your spending habits. You must record every cent you spend. The small expenditures can sabotage your efforts. (Read the parable in Luke 14:28-30 to learn the importance of working within our means.)

❀ *Do not make a budget—make a plan.*

Budgets do not work. With budgets, we create a list of how we want to spend our money, but not the real way it is spent. We need to set goals for ourselves that we can attain (e.g. pay off half of one credit card by the end of the year).

Determine the priority and necessity of your purchases. *Needs* include food, clothing, housing, and other basics. *Wants* are the choices about the quality of goods—steak or hamburger, new or used car. *Desires* are the things that we can afford only after we have met all of our obligations, both spiritual and material.

Be careful to spend wisely and keep accurate records. Going into debt for housing or a car is legitimate if it is covered by a payment contract and if the note's conditions are faithfully met. A word of caution: stay away from risky investments and too-good-to-be-true, get-rich-quick schemes. These will hinder, not help, your financial recovery. Some have run up a high credit-card debt or even lost their retirement funds when taken in by promises of a quick return on their money. (Read Proverbs 28:22.)

❀ *Do not expect instant miracles.*

You did not accumulate your debt in a day's time, and you will not pay it off instantly either. Stay focused and patient. After allowing for necessities, focus on paying off the highest interest accounts first. You can make smaller or minimum payments on lower interest accounts. As one high interest account is paid off, focus on the next highest. This maximizes the money that you have for debt reduction by paying down the most costly balances quicker.

Stick to your plan until you reach your goal. When you have achieved even one goal in clearing your debt, you will have a feeling of accomplishment in a job well done.

❀ *Save.*

Plan to save some money, no matter how small the amount, while you are working your way out of debt. If you save the money from one fast-food meal per week, at an average of $5 per meal, you will have $260 by the end of the year. Do you stop by the snack machines at work each day for a soft drink or candy? Or frequently have a cappuccino? By reducing your snack-buying by $7 per week—a low $1 per day—you can put another $364 in the bank. (And think of the added benefit of those saved calories!) Start somewhere. Small amounts add up quickly and the interest compounds.

❀ *Do not cosign on a loan.*

One area in which some have unintentionally gotten into trouble is by cosigning a loan for a family member or friend. Be sure to weigh the consequences carefully—regardless of how close the relationship/friendship. This means that *you* have promised to repay the debt if the borrower cannot. Unless you are prepared to repay the loan if the borrower defaults, you should never cosign any loan. Your credit rating is at stake if you do. Ask yourself why the person needs a cosigner. (Read Proverbs 6:1-5; 11:15.)

Avoid Easy Debt Triggers

What is a debt trigger? It is anything that causes you to jump, reflexively, for your credit card. Have you ever placed a catalog order and been asked by the sales person if you want to consider other sale items? They will try to persuade you to purchase items that you had no intention of buying when you first called! If we are not careful, we can add a lot of debt to our credit cards. These are known as *debt triggers:*

- ❀ Sales
- ❀ Department store credit cards
- ❀ Catalogs and online shopping
- ❀ Easy credit cards

Make a pact with yourself before shopping that you will buy only what you planned to purchase.

How Do You Rate?

Do you know that a bad credit rating may prevent you from making major purchases such as cars or a home? Or even taking a vacation? Your credit rating is available, whether good or bad. When you apply to make a credit purchase, the company can obtain your credit rating in a matter of minutes.

Everyone should check his credit report annually. If you have recently been turned down for credit, you are entitled to receive the report free of charge. Otherwise, the cost is about $10-15.

Be sure the report is accurate; errors do happen. If you have any questions, call the credit departments of the relevant companies and ask for an explanation of anything you do not understand. Look for notices of late payments. Also check that no one else's debt has been erroneously posted to your report because of a clerical error or someone with the same or similar name.

Card companies do not want competitors to steal their customers, so some will not report a good customer's on-time payment history to a credit bureau. Check a few months before applying for a mortgage to see if your good payment record is being noted.

Especially be alert for identity theft, a rapidly growing problem that can cause untold headaches in getting your records straightened out and your credit back in good standing. Do not just toss old bills and bank statements in the trash. Shred them. Even those credit card offers that come so frequently in the mail should be shredded before tossed. Otherwise, someone else may apply in your name.

Your credit rating is like gold; guard it with as much discipline as you can.

Credit Cards: Friend or Foe?

Even though credit cards can get us into trouble, there are some good reasons to have one. Holding one card and paying off the balance on time helps you to establish a credit history. You may also need a card for travel expenses or emergencies. Other than these reasons, credit-card spending needs to be kept at an absolute minimum.

Credit card companies do not like consumers who pay off their balance every month. This means less profit for them. Many of these companies charge high percentages for the use of their cards, which they do not get if you pay the full amount when the bill is issued!

Credit cards are here to stay, but there are ways to win in the credit-card game. Following these rules will lead you to financial freedom:

❊ *Do not carry a balance.*

Carrying a balance means paying far more than you should for everything you place on your card. It is one of the fastest ways to fall deep into debt. A recent report stated that the average person has $6,000 in credit-card bills. One debt management company said that its average client holds six credit cards and is $18,000 in debt.

How much does it cost you to carry a balance on your credit card? Just $5,000 at 15 percent will cost $415 in interest if you pay it off within a year. But can you afford the $451 monthly payment that would take? Reduce your payment to $106 per month and now you are looking at a six-year repayment time—with the interest paid now a gigantic $2,612. That "bargain" you purchased just ended up costing 52 percent more.

❊ *Read everything*

Most people receive frequent credit-card offers. Check any offer very carefully. You may need a magnifying glass to read the fine print, but that small print may sign you up for credit-card insurance, life insurance, or disability insurance. Read! Read! Read! When you get your monthly statement, look the bill over carefully along with everything that may arrive in the envelope. Sometimes the terms of your card agreement are changed with as little as fifteen days notice. They often slip the notice into your monthly statement, where it often goes unread.

❀ *Avoid late fees.*

With one late payment you are immediately charged with a late fee, which then gives you a larger balance with the late fee added in. This in turn causes your monthly payment to go up too. The card issuer can decide with one late fee to raise your interest rate.

❀ *Shop around.*

Competition among credit card companies is fierce. Use this knowledge to get what you want. Often you can get a late fee waived or your interest rate lowered just by asking.

There is no reason to hold a credit card that has a high interest rate or a short grace period. Go "rate surfing." Get the interest rate you want and find a card with no annual fee. Compare rates and terms of several cards. This can easily be done on the Internet.

❀ *Stop spending.*

Ultimately, this will make the most difference in your financial life. Make it difficult to use your card; leave it at home. Another suggestion is to keep your credit card frozen in water (like an ice cube). When tempted to buy something on credit, you will have lots of time while your card thaws to think about whether it is a wise purchase. Financially healthy people do not use credit cards for borrowing money and paying it back at high interest rates. Neither do they buy things they cannot afford. Keep a card on hand for emergencies only.

I Am Already in Debt. Now What?

Credit-card spending plays havoc with rationality. It encourages impulse buying, bad mood buying (thinking that rewarding yourself will fix what is wrong), and grandiose buying (buying to make a false impression).

Following these simple suggestions will help you reduce your credit card debt:

Pay more than the minimum payment each month. If you ever hope to pay off your credit cards, you must pay on time or a finance charge will be added onto the total, creating a larger minimum payment for the next month—and a larger finance charge added to the total again if you do not pay it. Pay the same amount every month, disregarding the declining minimum amount due as shown on the monthly statement, until the debt is paid. As one debt is paid, take that payment and redirect it to the regular payment of the next debt in line.

Get a system for credit card debt reduction. You need your own deadline for paying bills each month. (Refer to software options mentioned earlier.)

Negotiate with credit card companies. The amount of credit card debt has made creditors realize that if they do not want people backing down from their obligations completely (in other words, if they want to get any money back), they have to make deals, like these:

- ❀ Scenario One: You tell the company collection department that you are having financial difficulty and need to have your interest rate lowered. They will ask, "What can you manage?" Tell them.
- ❀ Scenario Two: A credit card company has offered to pay off all your old credit card debt at nine percent if you switch. Call your old company and tell them what you have been offered. Ask if they can do better, and go with whichever is lowest.

If you have a limited budget for debt reduction, write letters to each creditor, acknowledging the situation and telling when you can begin repayment. They will appreciate your openness and will likely be a lot nicer to you. In turn, this will give you some breathing space. Dealing with—rather than hiding from—your difficulties will boost your bruised self-esteem.

If you have a limited budget for debt repayment, write down what you can pay each creditor each month. Stick with your plan.

When dealing with creditors, keep your cool. It will make you feel better. Remember that some creditors have been taught to be mean and nasty. Do not be intimidated. You have figured out a plan and are truly attempting to deal with your situation.

Finding Help

Depending on your circumstances, you will need to consider whether or not you can manage your debt reduction yourself or if you should seek professional help. For more detailed information on how to get out of debt, check at your local library or search the Internet. You can also go to a certified credit counseling or debt management agency. These are non-profit organizations, and they can help you decide on the plan that is right for you. Credit or financial counseling agencies should provide you with free information. There should be no minimum debt required. When dealing with these agencies, ask for their costs, credentials, and qualifications before you make a decision.

The "Easy" Answer May be the Wrong Answer

Some people think that filing for bankruptcy is the answer to their debt problem. If you are one of these, consider what happens: Your debts go into "automatic stay"—that is, they are frozen. Under U. S. bankruptcy laws there are two options: Chapter 7, called liquidation, where your assets are sold to pay off your creditors, and Chapter 13, known as "wage-earner" bankruptcy. In filing Chapter 13 there is no property loss and your trustee establishes a payment plan, usually from three to five years. While bankruptcy sounds easy, it is not the "quick fix" you may think. The Fair Credit Report Act allows bankruptcy information to stay on your record ten years, although some information may be removed after seven years. Remember, in God's sight, even if not the court's, you still owe your creditors.

The most important thing to remember is that going through bankruptcy does not change your money management habits. If you do not change your habits, you will find yourself in financial difficulty over and over again.

Learning to be Content

"Not that I speak in respect of want: for I have learned, in whatsoever state I am, therewith to be content" (Philippians 4:11). Many of us are reaching for something that is just beyond our grasp financially and in other ways. Some of life's happiest people do not have any of this world's goods, but they are more content than those who have attained great wealth and riches. Things do not make us happy; it is being content wherever God has planted us.

Consider this. Debt does not put you in control, it puts you in chains. *You* want to make the decisions about when and what you buy—and with money that is in your pocket, not money you hope to get in the future.

Christian author and speaker Larry Burkett, known for his many books and seminars on finances, believes that the way a Christian uses money is the clearest indicator of what his inside commitment is really like.

Summary

Whether you are now in debt and need a way out or you want to develop a plan as a preventive measure, the process is much the same. These steps summarize what we have learned in this chapter.

1. **Knowledge.** You must know your financial situation. Whom do you owe? How much do you owe? How much do you have to pay toward these debts? If your outgo exceeds your income, something must change immediately.

2. **A Plan.** What are you going to do to get out of debt? Spend less? Take a part-time job? Negotiate lower payments? Get outside help? You have decisions to make as you start to stabilize your finances.

3. **Self-discipline.** Once you have your plan, stick with it. Remember, you are doing with less now to have a better future. Keep your goal in sight. (And allow yourself the occasional treat so that you do not feel deprived and miserable.)

4. **Education.** Learn not just about money, but about yourself. What attitudes led to your financial problem? Do you try to "buy" acceptance by wearing the right clothes or driving the right car? Do you lack confidence or feel insecure? What skills or abilities do you have that will help you earn more?

5. **Action.** Once you learn about yourself and once you have developed your plan, get busy. Nothing can be accomplished without action.

Jesus spoke on matters of finance more than any other subject because He knew the snare of the love of money. It is important that we use the money that God has given us wisely and for His glory. If God cannot depend on us to thank Him and be content with what He permits us to have instead of complaining, and if He cannot depend on us to be faithful in tithes and offerings, why should He entrust us with more?

This little poem sums it all up.

> "It's not what you'd do with a million
> If riches should e'er be your lot,
> But what are you doing at present
> With the dollar and a quarter you got?"

CHAPTER SIX

My Husband Won't Go

MODELING CHRIST TO AN UNSAVED HUSBAND

Being a woman in this ever-changing world is to say the least quite challenging. Shuffling the various responsibilities that surround us as a wife and mother leaves little space for free time or simply relaxing. Statistics indicate that over the past century, the number of women that work outside the home has grown considerably. In 1900, 5.3 million women worked outside the home. This number increased to 18.4 million in 1950 and finally to 66 million in 2001.[1] Thus, we struggle to meet the criteria required to be "super mom." If we are honest with ourselves, we often feel that the seemingly impossible task of meeting these immense responsibilities just cannot be accomplished.

Thankfully, I have the assistance of a wonderful, godly husband and family to assure me that I am doing a good job. Our life is centered around the church. Rarely does a day pass that some "church" activity is not connected to our daily routine. However, it goes without saying that not everyone has this blessing. Some of our wonderful women live in quite different family atmospheres. As a pastor's wife, I watched repeated situations where godly mothers faithfully came to church, bringing their children to service after service, while the husband remained conspicuously absent. Yet, they continued to serve God and worshiped Him on a consistent basis. I have never been in this situation. Even so, I have prayed and reached with many wonderful women as they trusted the grace of God to change their home. In this short chapter, I trust you will receive renewed encouragement and advice to help you continue your pursuit of God's will.

Let Biblical Principles Guide You

God's Word is always a timely source for instruction and guidance. It gives strong scriptural principles for wives living with unsaved husbands. I Peter 3:1-2 says, "Likewise, ye wives, be in subjection to your own husbands; that, if any obey not the word, they also may without the word be won by the conversation of the wives; while they behold your chaste conversation coupled with fear."

The Word instructs us as wives to be "in subjection to your own husbands." This may not always be easy if the husband does not lead the household in a godly manner. The "conversation" that Peter talks about, however, does not refer to preaching, proverbially speaking, fire-and-brimstone sermons to the husband. In contrast, he says to live godly lives before these unsaved men.

The unsaved husband watches the life you live. He sees the attitude you display to both him and the children, and he may point out those visible moments of frustration that come into our lives from time to time. Perhaps a godly wife may hear the statement: "Oh, yeah. You're really a Christian, aren't you?" I would be the first to admit being far from perfection, and I feel certain the stress you may feel does at times express itself. Should this type of situation arise and your emotions get the best of you, simply apologize and tell him you regret getting upset. Accepting responsibility for wrong actions is not a simple task, but taking the initiative to "admit the wrong" will certainly have an affect on the way he sees you. When he notices the change in attitude, he will realize that something is different about your life. Hopefully, after the unsaved husband sees the way you conduct yourself, he will be interested in finding out what makes you the wonderful woman you are. Concentrate on being a witness by the life you live before him. Be a respectful and loving wife.

When I was a little girl, I remember a wonderful lady that attended our church. Her husband was unsaved, but she brought her children to church every service. And, oh, how she could worship! I can still see her hands raised, speaking in tongues and glorifying God. She was willing to do anything she could to assist in God's kingdom. She baked for the bake sales, worked at our Mexican dinners, made peanut brittle—well, you get the idea. Most of all, I remember her as my Sunday school teacher. She made God's Word come alive as she ministered to that classroom of children. She took us on class excursions and field trips. Most importantly, she helped pray me through to this Holy Ghost experience.

Yet her husband remained unsaved. Her children grew to adulthood. One son became a minister and her daughter became a minister's wife. Still her husband made no move toward God. Unfortunately, this gracious lady was diagnosed with cancer when she was around sixty years old. She fought valiantly to overcome this deadly disease, but God called her home to be with Him. I will never forget when my mom called and told me that her husband prayed through to the Holy Ghost not long after her death.

I trust you will not have to wait as long as this lovely lady, but I wanted to share this story with you in hopes of encouraging you not to give up on your man. This precious lady's consistent, godly life did win her husband.

The loudest message you preach is the life you live before your husband. While he may mock your efforts, never stop praying and living as a witness before him.

Beware Satan's Tricks

One other incident comes to mind, which should serve as a cautious reminder not to become sidetracked by the devil's game. While we were pastoring, a great lady with an unsaved husband attended our church. She and her four children were faithful to every service. Her husband was a sinful man. He was part of the drug scene, and she found out that he had been unfaithful to her several times. Yet, she continued to request prayer that he would turn his life over to God. She once told us that she had been warned not to marry him and because of her rebellion, she felt she was responsible to stay with him for better or worse.

To say the least, my faith was weak that he would ever find God. However, one service, he walked in the church door and eventually made his way to the altar where he found the saving power of God. But that is not the end of the story. I am not exactly certain what happened, but this godly lady gradually slacked off from her consistent faithfulness. She began missing a few services, and eventually it was only the husband coming with the children. I was baffled! I could not believe that after all this time of praying for her husband that she would backslide. Thankfully, God intervened and she did come back to church. When we talked with her, she said that she had been so used to being the godly leader in the home and had been so focused on constantly praying for her husband's salvation, that when he found God she felt she no longer had that much to pray about. Because her battle had been won, she did not realize the struggle was what had kept her close to God. Fortunately, they worked things out and now attend church together as a family.

Some may feel as the lady above that you married for the wrong reasons. It is difficult to take responsibility or admit making a wrong decision or choice. This is the point where leaning on God is crucial. When you are down or depressed, a feeling of hopelessness may surface causing anger or guilt to overwhelm you. You may think, "I've brought this on myself, so I have to live with it." Whatever the reason, and there are perhaps any number of reasons why, that you are married to an unsaved husband, please remember one important fact: God can use you where you are.

I hesitate to mention this aspect, but some of you may be in physically or mentally abusive relationships. Be certain to consult with your pastor for his advice and guidance. God has given us a pastor as a spiritual leader to help us when we face difficulties and heartaches. Perhaps you can find ways to cope with this potentially harmful situation and regain a clear perspective. It may be that only then can you attempt to rebuild your marriage. It is God's will that you be strong. It is God's will that you have joy and peace in your life and marriage. But we must rely on His strength.

Pray for the Heart of a Servant

If you are feeling hopeless, pray for a new understanding of His will for your life. Pray for a new heart for your spouse. Pray that you receive a fresh desire to become a servant that does not grumble or complain. Jesus Christ was a servant first of all. I heard one of our great ministers, J. T. Pugh, say that the greatest aspiration he could ever have was to be a servant to God and then to others. It is not an easy job to be a servant. We all tend in our earthly nature to want to be coddled and taken care of. If we are not careful, our focus will be more on someone serving us rather than following the example of Jesus as He served the disciples and washed their feet. Do not get me wrong. Every once in a while we do need some "tender loving care." There is nothing wrong with "taking a breather." However, in the final analysis, we should strive to live life in such a way that we really do live to serve. Galatians 4:7 says, "Wherefore thou art no more a servant, but a son, and if a son, then an heir of God through Christ." There are great rewards in being a servant.

Yes, I know your life may not be the easiest to live. But Jesus Christ gives hope to the hopeless. He can give peace to you, even though you may live in dire circumstances. Give Jesus a chance to help you. Give Him a chance to make you the kind of woman He wants you to be.

In today's world, it is not politically correct to be submissive. Our world focuses on women's rights and the feminist movement. However, we should submit to our husbands. If a woman lives by the principles of submission to her husband, the Bible gives words of confidence that the lost and unsaved husband can be won to God largely on the basis of the behavior of his wife. God instructs saved wives to be witnesses through their submissive spirits. I really believe that as a result of your sweet attitude, God will reward your efforts with His blessings and anointing. The reward can, and most likely will be, a husband's salvation. Many husbands are not given respect. Let them see your "pure behavior" coupled with respect. By your living a godly life, they will know that there is something within you that they do not see in the world. They will know that Jesus does make a difference.

Be patient as you pray for your husband's redemption. I will say it again—the most compelling message you will ever provide is the life you live before him. Make church sound like the greatest and most exciting place to be. Do not dissect the pastor, the Sunday school superintendent, or any other leadership in the church in the husband's presence. He certainly will not want anything to do with something you criticize. Instead, talk about the good things. Paul tells us, "Whatsoever things are true, whatsoever things are honest, whatsoever things are just, whatsoever things are pure, whatsoever things are lovely, whatsoever things are of good report; if there be any virtue, and if there be any praise, think on these things" (Philippians 4:8).

God is aware that a marriage with a saved and an unsaved spouse will be difficult. His Word gives clear reason why believers should marry only believers (II Corinthians 6:14). However, it is possible to find yourself in the difficulty of an "unequally yoked" marriage. An unsaved husband and a saved wife are pulled in different directions. They will have different goals and different priorities. A Christian wife should be a better wife to her unsaved husband than the unsaved husband to the wife. She has a new nature because the Holy Ghost dwells in her. She has greater power than the husband. She should be less selfish. She should strive to manifest the fruit of the Spirit: love, joy, peace, patience, kindness, goodness, faithfulness, gentleness, and self-control (Galatians 5:22-23). She should be cognizant of his feelings about the church and try to work to help him not feel threatened about her church and church activities.

Examine Your Attitude

An unsaved husband may hold some animosity against the saved wife. Take time to consider his accusations very carefully. If the wife feels that there is some truth to them, ask him for forgiveness and start being the wife you should be. If you believe that you are being the Christian wife that you should be, ask God to soften the heart of your husband towards you and towards God. God is the One who tells us to submit. He is the One who will give us grace to work with the situation. It is God that can transform an unsaved husband into a saved husband if we will adhere to His Word.

I listened in awe at a recent youth convention as the minister related a story about a couple in his church. The lady had served the Lord for many years, praying that her husband would turn his life over to God. The husband eventually started coming to church activities but he made no move towards God. Then one day, while at a church picnic, the minister was called to the church to baptize a person who had just received the Holy Ghost. As he entered the auditorium, he reached out to pat the unsaved husband on the shoulder (who as well stood in the auditorium) and said, "How would you like to be baptized today?" To the minister's surprise, the man looked up at him and said, "Okay, I'm ready." He baptized this man in the wonderful name of Jesus! After seventeen years of much prayer, a godly lady finally saw her husband turn his life over to Jesus.

Do not give up on seeing the salvation of your husband. Your primary responsibility is to love God with all of your heart. Next, show your love by being a kind and submissive wife. Concentrate on being a witness by living a godly life before your husband. Make an effort to display a sweet and understanding attitude. Pray that you will receive a fresh desire to be a "servant" that does not grumble or complain. Let the power of the Holy Ghost strengthen you to the good in the life He wills for you in your home and marriage. And please, always remember the prayers of hundreds of thousands of Spirit-filled ladies are with you as you endeavor to lead your husband to the only saving name and plan ever given to this world.

Revival is here. In the words of General Superintendent Kenneth Haney, an irresistible wave is sweeping this world. May God grant you grace in your faithfulness to Him to see your husband be a part of this as well.

---

[1]www.aflcio.org/Factsaboutworkingwomen.cfm

WHEN YOUR HUSBAND IS NOT IN CHURCH
One Wife's Testimony

It's frustrating when your "better half" does not share the same belief in God as you. Some tips I have gained along the way include:

1. ***Never stop praying***—even when you feel like you are at your wit's end.

2. ***Know when to bite your tongue.*** I could think of several great retorts when my husband wanted to argue the validity of the gospel. However, I often felt that still small voice gently reminding me to keep silent.

3. ***Ask God to help YOU change.*** I became "high and mighty" at times with my husband and felt that root of bitterness take hold in my heart. But as the Spirit opened my eyes to my own weaknesses, I began to yield. As I confessed and asked God to help me change, I saw my husband, at the same time, begin to change (without him even realizing it).

4. ***Most importantly, never give up.*** God knows in advance what He has planned for you and your husband. Keep trusting in God. He can do what seems impossible!

> "In the same way, you wives must accept the authority of your husbands; even those who refuse to accept the Good News. Your godly lives will speak to them better than any words. They will be won over by watching your pure, godly behavior" (I Peter 3:1-2, NLT).

CHAPTER SEVEN

When a Child Rebels

CLAIMING GOD'S PROMISES FOR THE WAYWARD CHILD

*I*n a perfect world, gentle breezes breathe through screened windows, left open without fear. Nor is there any need to lock our doors while we sleep since crime is at zero. Gasoline is twenty-five cents per gallon; milk is eighteen cents per quart; bread is twenty-one cents a loaf; and divorce is almost non-existent. There are a few families with an alcohol problem, but they do not live on our street. Certainly everyone in our social circle or at our church lives a life of godliness. This is how it would be in a perfect world.

In the real world good people experience bad things. Righteous men and women must endure the horrific attack of Satan against home and family. I Peter 4:12 says, "Beloved, think it not strange concerning the fiery trial which is to try you, as though some strange thing happened unto you." These unexpected situations are intended as perfecting influences.

First of all, let us understand that God has our lives planned—start to finish! He knows exactly what we are going through. Yet, He does not allow the tempter's onslaught to destroy us, only to test our courage. Trials are meant to bring us closer to God. Temptation is intended to make us stronger, not weaker. When difficult things happen, God wants us to just hold on to Him. Satan is the author of confusion and will do all he can to cause trouble in the home. He especially targets our children because they are the most vulnerable. If he can win a generation, he will win the war.

What about My Child's Rebellion?

Parents have experienced life, and so they see the way more clearly than the child. Human nature will cause a child to want to experience life for himself. This often brings about rebellion in the heart of the child. Is not rebellion what the younger son in Luke chapter 15 manifest against his father's house? In spite of how much we know as parents, most children are going to withstand adults in one fashion or another at some time or other.

Rebellion may began with some minor issue, hardly a "heaven or hell" thing. Or it could be in ways so significant that their very soul is at stake. In either case, the godly parent must pattern his reaction after the manner of the prodigal's loving father. He never gave up believing that his son would return! He kept a wardrobe with all the needed apparel to lift his fallen child back to a level of honor within his family. The ring for his finger was a passport to restoration. His father had no desire to further destroy his son, only to have a right relationship with him.

When our children rebel, we must pray on! We must not have the attitude that they deserve to be shunned and should be cast away. That was the attitude of the older brother, *not* the loving father. His desire was for the lost to be found, the dead to live again. He longed for the restitution of his son, not only to his house but also to a higher standard of living and the fellowship of the community. He wanted the neighbors to experience the revival that existed in his home. When our children rebel, there must still be a foundation of hope for something good to come of it all. Rejoicing should not only be in heaven with the angels when one sinner repents but also among the saints in the congregation.

Welcoming the Prodigal

The prodigal son would have been in trouble had he met his older brother first as he made his way back home. His brother left him no room for recovery. He was less willing than the neighbors to give his prodigal brother a second chance. There must always be room in our hearts for an erring child to be restored. No one will love them like the parent loves them; and if that love is missing, where will they turn?

Oh, what joy when a rebellious child finds forgiveness from God and new opportunity with his family and fellowman! If it has not happened, we must keep the faith. We will reap in due season if we do not faint.

The words of Jesus should apply in dealing with errant children as well as others who have sinned. Matthew 18:21-22 tells us: "Then came Peter to him, and said, Lord, how oft shall my brother sin against me, and I forgive him? till seven times? Jesus saith unto him, I say not unto thee, Until seven times: but, Until seventy times seven."

We must not give in to the pressure of being overly concerned about what others will think when they learn of a child's failure. This is often a matter of pride on our part. We should be hurt because God has been offended, not because our own ego has been deflated by our failure to be recognized as the perfect parent.

Stand up to the accusations of Satan and declare by faith the promises in the Word of God. Isaiah 43:5-7 gave a beautiful promise of restoration: "Fear not: for I am with thee: I will bring thy seed from the east, and gather thee from the west; I will say to the north, Give up; and to the south, Keep not back: bring my sons from far, and my daughters from the ends of the earth; even every one that is called by my name: for I have created him for my glory, I have formed him; yea, I have made him." We realize this promise was to the children of Israel, but since we are of the household of faith by the promise of God, we can also apply those promises which were given to Israel to our situations.

Recovery can be just as beautiful as constancy. We must not surrender our faith in a moment of struggle. If we should give up on our own children, then who will hold them up in faith? If we stop believing, who will stand in the gap for them? Conditions always worsen when parents become negative and opinionated regarding a wavering child. According to Isaiah 54:17, "No weapon that is formed against thee shall prosper." Drugs, alcohol, illicit sexual conduct, or any such thing cannot be stronger than the steadfast prayer of a faithful parent. Keep believing! Never stop praying and never give up in the spiritual fight for your child.

The parents of Moses are listed in the eleventh chapter of Hebrews because they stood strong for the life of their child in the face of the pharaoh's decree. We must not waver; rather we must remember that with God all things are possible to them that believe.

Why should our children be lost when others are returning to the fold? God loves one child as much as He loves another. He has not sworn a vendetta against our house. By faith we are the seed of Abraham and are to inherit God's promises to us and to our children throughout all generations.

What if Jochebed had said, "I am only a woman and the law of the land commands me to surrender my son to the deadly law of Egypt"? She did not accept the fate of the king's decree when he commanded that all the sons of the Israelites should be slain. Hebrews 11:23 states that by faith they were not afraid of the king's commandment. She steadfastly defied the decree in order to preserve the life and hope of her son.

If we operate out of fear, we will go from defeat to defeat. Our testimony will be one of woe and misery. We must stand up to our fears and take the victory over them. Fear has torment. King David said, "What time I am afraid I will trust in thee." Do not concentrate on fear and uncertainty. Get into and believe the Word of God. This is not about who is to blame. Satan is the accuser! You love your child. Take action according to the Word and hold fast to the promises found there.

Two Mothers, Two Responses

Our children can, and do, make bad choices. When they do, we must insist that they take responsibility for their own actions. They must be responsible for their choices and at the same time be accountable for the results of those choices.

Three teenagers once got into trouble with the leadership of the church. It was at first a minor childish behavior which was reprimanded. The three youngsters were called to task by the pastor. One mother brought her child to see the pastor and repented with tears for her child's participation in the misconduct. She sought forgiveness for the child and herself alike. Perhaps she had not been careful to instruct this child in certain matters as she ought. Whatever the case, she wanted proper restitution for her child. She insisted that repentance be made on the part of the youngster. The child wept and confessed, and from that day a transformation came about in his spirit and attitude. He has become a spiritually strong young adult and holds a responsible position in the church.

The other two children were never repentant. They and their parents made the decision that leadership had no authority over their lives and bad manners in this matter. Sad to say, they eventually left the protection of the church and sought a worldly path for their lives.

The Bible teaches us that we should "train up a child in the way he should go: and when he is old, he will not depart from it" (Proverbs 22:6). The Christian young man was taught good manners, to respect leadership, and to be sensitive to the Spirit of God through repentance when an error was made. He was taught that he should be accountable and responsible for his own actions. If a child has been taught the ways of life according to the Word of God and errs in the way, you as a parent have done your best and must simply hold to the promise that he will not depart from his teaching. When he is ready to turn his heart again to God, he will know the way.

There is a saying that "if children are disciplined when you can do it with a broom-straw, they will never become so unruly that you are forced to use a ball bat." Times have changed, and with them so have methods of correction. One thing remains constant: "A child left to himself bringeth his mother to shame" (Proverbs 29:15).

How Do We Teach Responsibility?

How do we teach our child to be responsible for his own actions? Life training varies very little from case to case. Personalities may vary from child to child. But the standard of conduct in the home must be consistent. Life-long lessons are not matters of brevity! They are meticulously rehearsed over and over until well learned. They are taught repeatedly until they are nature.

So it is with our children. Life lessons should be long taught and well learned. Teach them to honor God, their country, and their parents. God in turn will honor them. God loves them unconditionally, but He will not honor them unless they do righteously. If a child is taught and learns proper respect of parents and leadership early in life, it will automatically develop self-esteem. He or she will be in fellowship and favor with God and man. Luke tells us that "Jesus increased in wisdom and stature, and in favour with God and man" (Luke 2:52). Jesus grew and developed both physically and spiritually, fully aware of God's will. Notice that it said that He grew in favor with God and man. We can do no better than to teach our children how to deal with God and man. Jesus is certainly our finest example. We must teach our children early the importance of a born-again experience so that they will have power to overcome the deceptions of Satan.

Knowledge of the Word of God and being filled with His Spirit will help a child to develop self-esteem. When a child has a reasonable level of self-esteem, he will better rise to life's challenges. Success in any area of life, especially in the area of being a strong Christian, is more readily achieved when they are taught to have personal confidence.

A recent article stated that many, if not most, abuses of addictive natures are a product of lost or low self-esteem. When adults are heavy-handed and abusive toward children, the child's self-esteem is destroyed. If parents are overtly severe in their treatment of their children (or toward their spouse), they will gradually wear away that child's self-esteem.

It is sad to see a child after abuse has stripped away confidence and self-esteem. Our lives are not shielded from the heinous crimes against children simply because we are Christians. We must be vigilant and pray against any evil which comes against our children whether or not they are in good standing with the family and the church.

We Must Love Unconditionally

Regardless of the reason a child has gone away from godly teaching, he must find that we not only read and quote Scripture but also that we live it from the heart. We cannot condone the sin of our child, but neither should we treat him as though he is the enemy. We must love him back to God as surely as we would try to win any sinner. It is sin that God hates—not the sinner.

We can through prayer change the world around us. The love of God is shed abroad in our hearts by the Holy Ghost. That love will reach just as Christ reached when He gave His life on the cross. John 3:16 summed it up this way: "For God so loved the world, that he gave." He gave and we must give, not just in words but in actions. The old saying, "Actions speak louder than words," is true. We must do more than just pray for our children. We must put our love into action and show them that we love them as much as Christ loved us "while we were yet sinners."

We may find this difficult to do if our own egos have been offended by the actions of our children, but Christ loved unconditionally. Can we do less? One child lost is too many. We must never care for others who are lost more than we care for our own children. The lost child who feels that no one cares is a tragedy for him and the family.

The only answer is the altar. We must stay on the altar. Joel 2:17 states: "Let the priests, the ministers of the LORD, weep between the porch and the altar, and let them say, Spare thy people, O LORD, and give not thine heritage to reproach, that the heathen should rule over them: wherefore should they say among the people, Where is their God?"

Joel 2:23-29 tells us: "Be glad then, ye children of Zion, and rejoice in the LORD your God: for he hath given you the former rain moderately, and he will cause to come down for you the rain, the former rain, and the latter rain in the first month.

"And the floors shall be full of wheat, and the vats shall overflow with wine and oil. And I will restore to you the years that the locust hath eaten, the cankerworm, and the caterpillar, and the palmerworm, my great army which I sent among you.

"And ye shall eat in plenty, and be satisfied, and praise the name of the LORD your God that hath dealt wondrously with you: and my people shall never be ashamed.

"And ye shall know that I am in the midst of Israel, and that I am the LORD your God, and none else: and my people shall never be ashamed.

"And it shall come to pass afterward, that I will pour out my spirit upon all flesh; and your sons and your daughters shall prophesy, your old men shall dream dreams, your young men shall see visions:

"And also upon the servants and upon the handmaids in those days will I pour out my spirit."

These are the promises of God for us, straight from His Word. We are promised repeatedly that the shame shall be removed from among us; that "my people shall never be ashamed." We must not as God's people allow Satan to intimidate us—to attack us and make us fear him. God's will is clearly defined throughout the Scriptures. Nowhere is His purpose more clear than in II Peter. 3:9: "The Lord is not slack concerning his promise, as some men count slackness; but is longsuffering to us-ward, not willing that any should perish, but that all should come to repentance." Recovery is the heartbeat of God, so it must be our heartbeat. God loves and longs for the lost; so must we. He desires to restore all that was lost; so we will also desire to restore those who are lost.

We Must Pray, Love, and Believe

What, then, must we do when a child rebels? We will pray without ceasing for that child. And how will we respond to the need of that child? Respond in the same manner in which the Lord responds to us—by loving our child. We will love even the one which deserves love least, because in all likelihood that one needs love most and God loved us before we ever returned His love.

We will trust in the Lord with all our might, for He knows the end of a matter from the beginning. While going through a trial of faith for our errant child, we will believe in the Lord. We will refuse guilt over the wrong choices our children have made, and we will worship God always for that is the right choice on our part. We know that through it all He is with us; of what then shall we be afraid?

We will thank God for the signs of a tender heart in our child. We will praise Him for His Word because it is forever settled in heaven and it is not His will that any should perish. We will stand in the gap between our child and God through intercessory prayer until our child is restored to a right relationship to our heavenly Father.

Claim the words of Jeremiah 31:16-17 as a personal promise of the wayward child's return: "Refrain thy voice from weeping, and thine eyes from tears: for thy work shall be rewarded, saith the LORD; and they shall come again from the land of the enemy. And there is hope in thine end, saith the LORD, that thy children shall come again to their own border."

IF YOUR FRIEND'S CHILD REBELS

What can you do or say when a friend's child has rebelled? If your friend chooses to confide in you, there are several things that you can do to encourage her.

1. Above all else, listen. Do so without assigning blame or judging. Just listen.
2. Keep everything told you in strict confidence. Do not share, even as a prayer request, what she confides to you.
3. If it is a one-time incident of irresponsibility, help her to view it in the proper perspective. She and her husband can set proper boundaries without over-reacting to the situation.
4. Encourage her to seek godly counsel to learn how to deal with the situation.
5. Remember that every family is different. What is appropriate for your family may not work in hers.
6. Remind her that the child will always be her son/daughter.
7. Pray together for wisdom.
8. Remind her frequently that there is always hope.

CHAPTER EIGHT

When the Honeymoon is Over

COPING IN AN UNHAPPY MARRIAGE

Are you thinking that the glass slipper was not such a perfect fit after all? Maybe the fairytale did not go the way you planned, and your Prince Charming has lost his charm. If your dream of the "happily-ever-after" looks more like a nightmare today, do not lose heart. After all, marriage is not a fairytale; it is full of real life challenges, hard work, and sacrifice. Following sound biblical concepts may help turn your marriage around so that you can enjoy its blessings and rewards too.

It Is God's Will for Your Marriage to Work

After the honeymoon is over and you reach some bumps in the road, it can be tempting to say, "I made a mistake; this is not God's will for my life." Some may remember with regret that good advice was ignored in the excitement of dating and romance. In hindsight you may recall red flags or warning signs to which you should have reacted. Maybe marriage to the man who is now your husband *was not* God's perfect will for you at that time.

Many women in the church today were married before coming to God. You may say, "If only I'd have known God back then, I would have made a completely different decision." Or maybe everything started out perfectly for you only to come apart at the seams later. No matter how it happened, no matter what your story, because of the vow you took before God it is now His will that you do what you can to make your marriage work.

The wisdom of the world today is to divorce and remarry at the first sign of trouble. God's wisdom is to give your best effort to save the marriage you are in. The Bible description of the last days, "marrying and giving in marriage," refers to our day of multiple marriages. What began as a Hollywood phenomenon has become an accepted way of life for many.

As we were growing up and heard of yet another couple divorcing, my mother would caution her children: "People can spend their lives trading one set of problems for another. They often find themselves in a far worse situation than the one of which they traded out." As a little girl, I thought my mother was pretty smart! Today, I have an even better understanding of how profound her advice was.

As life has its seasons, so does marriage. You vowed to take him "for better, for worse, for richer, for poorer, in sickness and in health." The truth is, if you live long enough, in the course of your marriage you are likely to see some of it all. After surviving the hard times, the good times will be even better!

Look at Yourself

You are not responsible for what your husband does. You are responsible to God for how you react to what he does and for what you do. You cannot always change his behavior, but you can work on your own. When things are not going right, look at yourself first. Is there an area where you could be doing better?

Am I patient with my husband? Am I kind to him? Do I feel envious when things go his way? Do I show a proud, arrogant spirit? Am I vain and stubborn with him? Am I selfish in the marriage? Do I always want my way? Am I overly sensitive and easy to offend? Have I learned to forgive and forget? (Adapted from I Corinthians 13.)

Generally, most marriage problems are not just one person's fault. Usually, both people share some of the blame!

In marriage we need to celebrate and appreciate the good times. Work with your husband's strong points. Why did you fall in love with him in the first place? What attracted you to him in the beginning? Ask the Lord to help you see those qualities in him again. Do not focus on all of the negatives. Someone said, "You become what you focus on." If you focus on being unhappy and miserable, you will always be unhappy and miserable! If you focus only on the problems in your marriage, that is all you will be able to see. I certainly do not want my husband to be blind to my good qualities and see only my faults and deficiencies. I owe him the same courtesy.

Get a Life!

You need to develop some outside interests in your life. Volunteer at your child's school. Stay active in your church. Find your talents and get busy working in the kingdom! Teaching a Sunday school class, singing in the choir, or taking part in street evangelism will lift your spirits and ward off depression. Living an active full life will keep you balanced and your problems in perspective.

Fifty/Fifty Isn't Enough

Every marriage requires hard work and effort, mixed in with a lot of give and take. If you both look at it as a fifty/fifty proposition, expecting to give no more than fifty percent all of the time, there will be nowhere to meet in the middle and you will end up in a standoff. Each one has to be willing to give more than his or her share. Then you can meet in the overlap! Ideally, it should not always be the same one who does all of the giving or all of the taking. There will be times when your husband gives one hundred percent and other times when you give one hundred percent. Other times there will be a sixty/forty balance, or thirty/seventy. Love will not always feel the need to keep score. A little maturity will go a long way. I am an adult; I am not the princess. I will not always get my way. I am not the only person who counts in this marriage!

Look to Jesus!

An important key to surviving in a troubled marriage is to find your happiness and fulfillment in God. Make Him your center and focus. Strive to please God and look to Him for love and approval. We all need to do this anyway, but married women often tend to make their husbands their center. In a dysfunctional marriage, it is imperative to your spiritual, mental, and emotional health to get your validation from God. If you and your husband are having problems and you look to him for your sense of worth, you may be sorely disappointed and end up feeling like a failure. Look first to Jesus as the source of all you need; He will not disappoint! When life is great, a lot of people easily settle for a superficial relationship with God, just doing enough to feel saved. Times of adversity, especially in marriage, will force us to desperately seek God. Adversity, as painful as it is to go through, will lead us into a deeper, richer experience with God, if we look to Him for help.

Follow *His* Example

The Bible compares the marriage relationship to the relationship between God and His church. It is in passing through the hard times that we are able to understand more profoundly the love of God. When your spouse does something that deeply hurts and offends, you have an opportunity to get to know more of Jesus "and the fellowship of His sufferings" (Philippians 3:10). When you see how difficult it is to forgive, pass over that fault, and go on loving, you get a glimpse of the grace of God. How many times have we offended Him, even embarrassed or made Him ashamed of us—and His love and mercy were there anyway? Can you show that same love of God to your husband? Forgiving, especially when it is hard to do—especially when the other person does not seem to deserve it—keeps God's mercy flowing unhindered in your life. Forgiveness, given out of a pure desire to please God, is very powerful; it opens the door for Him to take up your cause and defend you!

Do Not Let Bitterness Take Root

Women can have very long memories. We have all known the woman who can stand at the sink washing dishes and revisit her husbands past offenses point by point. She may remember something that happened *last month, last year, or five years ago!* Fresh tears drop into the dishwater and she is angry and offended all over again. If her husband happens to walk in during this ritual, he will never know what hit him! Do not be her. Bitterness will rot your soul and sicken your spirit. When you make a decision to forgive, keep praying until you can let go of the offense. It may take more than one prayer session. Then, do not let yourself take it up again. Do not indulge in that pity party where you replay it over and over. Do not keep talking about it. After God forgives, rejoice that He

91

forgets our sins. We do not have to worry about Him bringing them up anymore. Once something is under the blood, it is gone forever! Oh, to be more like Him!

Be Careful to Whom You Talk

Be loyal. As a general rule it is not a good idea for you to complain about your husband to other people. He deserves the same privacy that you want. (You do not want him complaining about you to everyone, do you?) If your situation is such that you need to talk to someone, be careful in choosing the person in whom you will confide. Do not go to someone who does not like your husband. The person might enjoy being entertained with soap-opera installments of your trials and tribulations. It is true that this person will give you abundant sympathy; but sympathy and good advice can be two different things. "I'd never put up with that." "He's such a jerk." "How do you stand it?" I'd be out of there in a minute!" "You poor thing." "I feel so sorry for you." This kind of sympathy will make you weak and put you into a negative mindset. You will feel like a victim and therefore be justi-fied in stomping around the house with a bad attitude.

Instead, talk to someone who will be honest with you, someone who wants to see your marriage succeed. A friend who will listen and pray with you, without passing judgment, may be just what you need to help you over a rough spot.

Children in a Troubled Home

God has entrusted you and your husband with the care of your children. They are innocent and must be protected. When children see conflict between the two people they love the most, it is frightening and confusing. Do not use your children as weapons to hurt each other. They do not want to be caught in the middle of their parents' problems. Children should not be asked to take sides and chose one parent over the other. Do not degrade their daddy to them; remember that they love him. As much as possible, do not let them witness screaming, fighting, and insults. It shakes to the foundation, resulting in feelings of insecurity. If your children do see you fight, let them see you make up. Answer their questions with honesty. They are smarter than you realize and can feel tension in the home. If you are not honest with them and do not acknowledge what is happening, they may think that the problems are their fault. Reassure your kids and explain, "Mommy and daddy disagree right now, but they both still love you." We know the emotional damage that can be done to children living in a dysfunctional home. They can be scarred for life and suffer terrible consequences for things over which they had no control. Work with your husband to provide the best possible emotional environment for your children. They are counting on you. If you do not protect them, who will?

A Godly Mother Can Make a Difference

We would all like to be able to raise our children in a perfect environment, but life does not always go according to our plan. Sometimes we find ourselves in difficult circumstances through no fault of our own. Be encouraged; a loving, godly mother can make a world of difference to her children. I grew up in a home where alcohol was abused. We saw and heard things that no child should witness. My mother never received the Holy Ghost, but she feared God and sought Him for help. I cannot explain it, but somehow, in the midst of all the turmoil, she made us feel loved and protected.

My mother never let us disrespect our father. She constantly told us that he loved us and she praised his good qualities. She let us know that it was the alcohol talking, not his heart. With honesty, she eased the sting of cruel words. She helped us to see and love the man behind the alcohol. We saw her cry and we saw her pray. Then we shared the joy when, after more than twenty years, my father found freedom from his alcohol addiction. I am not saying that we did not pay any consequences for the life we lived, but with the help of God, my mother guided her children through a desperate situation and helped them come out of it as responsible adults. She did her best, trusted God, and that made the difference. She was our hero. God is able to use you, too, to keep your children from harm.

When Love Hurts

Love should not hurt! Domestic violence is a growing problem in our country, especially among the younger generation. Boyfriend abuse is now widely accepted by teenage girls, as is the spousal abuse that follows. Abuse in any of its various forms is never acceptable. God's Word instructs husbands to love their wives as their own bodies. We do not see men giving themselves black eyes, or breaking their own ribs!

"It's your fault." "You made me do it". "You provoked it." "If you would just change." These excuses do not justify violent abusive behavior. It is *not* your fault! He has a serious problem that must be addressed. If you and/or your children are living in an abusive situation, I urge you to seek qualified help right away. God does not expect you to do the impossible. He wants you and your children to be safe. Love should not hurt. Tell your sons, tell your daughters, love should not hurt!

Pray for Your Marriage

Appeal to the highest authority for help. Pray daily for God's blessings on your marriage. Pray that God will give needed wisdom to both of you as husband and wife. Ask Him to let you see your own mistakes, then ask for forgiveness for the mistakes you have made. Claim all of the Bible's promises that apply to you. If you feel like you and your husband are now enemies, Proverbs 16:7 promises that "when a man's [or a woman's] ways please the LORD, he maketh even his enemies to be at peace with him." Claim that peace for your home and ask God to help you fall in love all over again. He wants to bless you. Just ask!

In Conclusion

Just as people are different, every marriage is different. There is no one-size-fits-all fix that will apply to every marriage. The Word of God is the only counsel that always applies. Read it, study it, and live it. Be honest and sincere with each other; do not be afraid to seek help when you need it. Be encouraged in this: when we have done our best, when we have sought after Him, He will be there to help.

CHAPTER NINE

Instant Family Without Instant Love

CHALLENGES OF THE BLENDED FAMILY

She leaned forward, elbows resting on her knees, her brown eyes wide with shame and horror. In a whisper, almost silently, her lips framed the words, *"I hate being married and I hate his children."*

Kelly was a newly married stepmother. At thirty-five she had done well in the corporate world and had achieved a successful career. She was also active in her church, singing in the choir and teaching a Bible study class. Her vivacious personality and quick wit made her a favorite with co-workers and church family alike. She had met Chad at a church concert and married him after dating five months. Now, eight months into the marriage she was seeing me for individual counseling. Chad did not know she was here.

Because of sin, we live in a world where death and divorce step into hearts and homes, tearing families apart. Some family situations result from sin or wrong choices before a person became a Christian; some result from sin or wrong choices after a person became a Christian; and some result from tragedies beyond a person's control. Regardless of the reasons or of past rights and wrongs, these marriages and families need help, and it is God's will for them to function properly and be successful. This chapter was written to address this need, which is very real in our world today where "more than half of all first marriages end in divorce; second marriages do worse, failing at a rate of about 60 percent" (Gottman, p16).

For the newlywed couple, remarriage most likely includes children on the part of one or both of the partners. The time to blend and bond, work out life choices, couples issues, personal preferences, and parenting styles does not exist. The couple enters the marriage facing a multitude of stressors from day one. How will the individuals in the relationship manage?

There is great instability in remarriages and the divorce rate continues to climb. Like Kelly and Chad, few couples choose pre-marital counseling and enter into the marriage with unrealistic expectations and limited knowledge of stepfamily issues.

Marriage therapists agree that there are twenty major issues in remarriage families. All of these issues are cited as potential triggers of crisis in remarriages. They are:

Issue 1: Name for the New Parent

What do I call her? Titles do make a difference in how people are perceived and treated in relationships. Probably the best advice is what *not* to do. This is only an issue if titles are forced onto people who are resistant to them. Do not insist on being called "Mom" or "Dad." Do not imply by words or silence that you are a biological parent of a stepchild. Do not feel awkward about being steps—the families need to work out what is right for each member of the unit.

Issue 2: Affection for the New Parent and the Absent Parent

Love and loyalty can get all jumbled up. *Is it possible to love Dad's new wife and remain loyal to Mom? If I care about my step-dad will my real dad feel hurt?* These are questions asked by children of all ages, even adult children, in remarried families. Families should explore the ability to love and remain loyal to many individuals in our lives. Parents and stepparents need to give permission to children to maintain parental loyalty as well as stepparent loyalty and the freedom to express feelings of love or affection when they are ready and how they choose.

Issue 3: Loss of the Natural Parent

Couples and their children are building new relationships and lives on the destroyed dreams or shattered vows of previous marriages. The past always influences the present. The debate rages, "Which Hurts Worse—Death or Divorce?" Individuals who have lost at love feel the pain of rejection, guilt, and failure. The spouse who lost a partner in death struggles with the helplessness of love being snatched away, leaving them raw and bleeding. In the end, whether the marriage ends because of death or divorce, everybody hurts. Tragic endings to marriages leave scars. Death and divorce both create fear to love again.

Too often, while in this stricken and vulnerable condition, a person will purposely seek a new partner rather than do the necessary work of healing and dealing with loneliness. While in grief, people take steps that they may have never considered. Time is vital in order to make balanced decisions regarding the future. Individuals and family units need:

❀ time to grieve

❀ time to heal

❀ time to readjust attitudes and lifestyles without the former spouse

❀ time to prayerfully focus on the future

❀ time for decisions to be made based on healthy mental attitudes

❀ time for the bereaved to see the potential partner as the person he or she is, not as a replacement for the spouse who was lost

No one can do what time can. The Bible clearly states, "To every thing there is a season, and a time to every purpose under the heaven" (Ecclesiastes 3:1). This passage defines the seasons and times of life. There are definite times for rejoicing, but there must also be a time of mourning.

Issue 4: Instant Love of New Family Members

An instant family does not equal instant feelings of love. It takes time to form emotional bonds and sometimes bonding never occurs. Why do adults believe because they have fallen in love that they will love each other's children? Why do couples expect love between all the children in the remarriage? It is a hope. *Love me, love my child* is the unspoken expectation. When this expectation remains unfulfilled, disappointment and anger set in. Yet, it is unrealistic to expect instant love.

There are many personal and societal expectations for instant love in the new family. Mothering and the associated feelings of love and nurturing are seen as something that should come naturally to women; yet, many women—like Kelly—are dismayed when they do not experience feelings of love or affection for their stepchildren. Women face the paradoxical situation of being seen as the evil or wicked stepmother while still being expected to love and mother the children marriage has brought into her life. These polar opposite views are difficult for a person to adjust to. How is a woman to pull this off? It seems women, more than men, tend to enter second marriages or marry a partner for whom it is a second marriage with the high and unrealistic expectations of being the family savior. She is more likely to burnout than a stepfather who research indicates moves slower into the parenting role.

Issue 5: Fantasy about the Old Family Structures

Children of divorce fantasize that *one day* mom and dad will reconcile. The fantasy is invaded by reality in the form of a new mate. These children struggle when parents remarry. "A divorced father's nuptials are often tougher. Even adult children may nurse the fantasy that their family may someday be whole again; dad's remarriage destroys that dream. 'I felt like I was catapulted into a nightmare,' says Stasi, 29, a school teacher in Boston. 'When Dad got remarried, it made me feel like my family didn't exist anymore.'" No matter what the circumstances of the divorce were or the ages of the family members, it seems there is the hope that *mom and dad will work this out and I will have my family again.* The new stepparent is an intrusion. It is very difficult to bond with a resented intrusion.

Issue 6: Discipline by the Stepparent

After the honeymoon, the happy couple returns to establish a family structure by blending existing structures. This task is fraught with challenges and difficulties. The number one problem listed in much of the research on stepfamilies is discipline. There are three types of stepparent discipline:

❀ inattentive and disengaged

❀ actively involved and overly restrictive

❀ tentative as if "walking on eggshells"

Most stepfamilies will fall into one of these types without intervention. Gender differences are evident at this time. It seems stepmothers move too quickly and stepfathers are too slow to assert themselves in family matters. Problems occur when a stepmother assumes an authoritative role when children do not yet recognize her as a valid family member. Problems also are present if the stepfather does not work with the mother to set consistent limits. To make the marriage stable, the parents must work together and reflect a united front to the children.

Issue 7: Confusion over Family Roles

There is much uncertainty over the roles, rights, and responsibilities of stepparents. While assuming the duties and obligations of the biological parent, the stepparent's rights remain ambiguous. They have the work of a biological parent without the privileges of parenting.

Children report confusion over roles when each household places them in a different category. For example, Monday through Thursday Lucy is an only child living with her doting single mother. This changes on Friday afternoon when she travels to her dad's household where she has a stepmother, two older stepbrothers, and three younger half-siblings.

Issue 8: Sibling Conflict

In blended families the hierarchy of the original unit is rearranged by the remarriage. It is crucial to the success of the new family for stepsiblings to have healthy respectful relationships. While love cannot be expected or required, respectful attitudes and ways of interacting should be a household policy. Parents should instruct in and model conflict resolution skills. If the tension is unbearable, a counselor may serve as the family mediator in the negotiation process of establishing the new household.

Studies indicate that the addition of a child after a remarriage may bring more harmony into stepsibling relationships. The new child is perceived as "the one we are all a part of." If the remarriage is not stable, having a child is ill advised.

Issue 9: Competition for Time

Everyone rivals for attention. The new husband wants intimate time with his lover while the stepchildren want mom all to themselves. His children from his previous marriage are jealous because the stepsiblings live in the same home with dad but they cannot. Parents need quality time with children, but couples need to remember to focus on each other. This balancing act is difficult, but not optional.

Issue 10: Extended Kinship Network

Who are the people who have an impact on the newly formed family? This system may include all former extended family members of both spouses, the remarriage family itself, and other non-family members. With the addition of each person, the greater the complexity of relationships and the stretch of resources to meet the needs and demands of each. Research shows moderate levels of contact with relatives is the optimal solution. The question then becomes, how do you determine "moderate"?

Issue 11: Sexual Conflicts

One of the most difficult issues with which remarriage family members deal is sexuality. There is great potential for inappropriate sexual behavior in a newly formed stepfamily. Families should be aware of the sexual boundaries required to maintain health in the home. The new parental couple, in the romantic stage of marriage, may be modeling sexuality, which is observed by the children. Stepsiblings may experience sexual feelings for each other and may "act like the adults." In the worst of cases, a sexual relationship may develop between the stepparent and stepchild related to the nature of the family, which is non-biological and short-termed, lacking the development of parent-child ties which would prevent such an occurrence.

Issue 12: Changes over Time

The verdict is still out over the time it takes for stepfamilies to organize and stabilize. Some have stood firm with a minimum of two years while others argue that it takes up to twelve years for stepfamilies to experience the same level of cohesiveness as a biological family. While the literature argues the length of time, it does seem to agree that the first two years of remarriage is a vulnerable time for all family members.

Issue 13: Exit and Entry of Children

Known by most as "visitation," the exit phase would be the Friday when the child would spend all day anxious or anticipating the weekend visit with the non-custodial parent. The entry phase begins when the child leaves the home of the non-custodial parent to return home. The child is affected before and after the visit, and it may be disruptive to the quality of life the child and home experiences.

Children of divorce live in a continual state of change. While it may be disruptive, children are much better off having visits with parents than not seeing them at all or infrequently.

Issue 14: Society's Concept of the Stepfamily

Although the nuclear family is still valued by our culture as the ideal, it is no longer the norm. Society often translates different as undesirable, and stepfamilies may be viewed as a negative family relationship. Numerous studies and reviews have found that there are generally negative stereotypes of stepfamilies.

The identity management work for stepmothers revolves around the effect of myths about stepfamily relations on stepfamily members in general and stepmothers in particular. For example, at least three of the Brothers Grimm's fairy tales—"Hansel and Gretel," "Cinderella," and "Snow White"—revolve around the actions of an evil stepmother. These stories may appear innocent, unless of course you happen to be a stepmother or a stepchild. These tales have a negative impact on the identity of the stepmother. The myth of the evil stepmother has been propagated through fiction of all types. Did you know that 345 versions of the "Cinderella" story exist?

Issue 15: Familial Self-Concept

The prefix *step* suggests a negative stereotype causing family members to see their family as different, inadequate, or deficient. A blended family must develop its own feeling of "we-ness" and traditions. Building a history together gives the family its own identity. It is critical for the new family to create new rituals and traditions. This may be done by building upon old favorites or doing something different and unique.

Issue 16: Individual Self-Concept

People will compare. Children compare, in-laws compare, out-laws (former in-laws) compare, friends compare, spouses compare, and we compare ourselves to each other.

Yet, God through His Word instructs us, "They measuring themselves by themselves, and comparing themselves among themselves, are not wise" (II Corinthians 10:12). A great gift to give each member of the new marriage and family is the gift of a fresh start with no comparisons. Do not compare verbally or mentally. Comparisons are never fair.

Issue 17: Effects of Parenting on the New Marital Relationship

Rather than being a process in marriage, marriage may interrupt or intrude upon the parenting ongoing with the children. The couple has not had the quality alone time before the arrival of the first child. They have not had the experience of uninterrupted time to bond. In the beginning, it may be necessary to focus on parenting issues and resolve them, but the couple still needs to focus on creating a "we." All of the marital energy should not be focused on parenting and problem solving.

Issue 18: Financial Concerns

Money must be divided among many responsibilities and loyalties. Older couples may have conflict over wills and the distribution of property. In younger couples, conflicts revolve around child support and/or alimony.

Money is a currency of power. It is also seen as a reflection of true priorities and commitments. Maybe it is based on the scriptural understanding that "where your treasure is, there will your heart be also" (Matthew 6:21). Life is not fair and everything cannot possibly be equitable one hundred percent of the time. The family should endorse the "common good" approach. When you cannot be equitable, be understanding.

Issue 19: Continuing Adult Conflict

Children are often caught in the middle of warring adults who have never resolved their problems. There are couples who are legally divorced but not emotionally divorced.

Feelings that exist after the breakup of the previous relationship may affect the current relationship and create difficulties. Struggles from the previous marriage may be played out in the interaction over the children and parenting issues. If adult conflict existed before a remarriage, it will flow into the new family unit.

Issue 20: Competition of the Non-Custodial Parent

The goal of the parents should be to keep the needs of the children first when dealing with the non-custodial parent. Research shows that, over time, visits with the non-custodial parent declines and contact becomes less frequent. It may be because of the stress related to parental conflict and unresolved marital disputes. It creates high levels of tension in children to be caught between warring parents using the child as a form of revenge.

These are the issues seen by families and counselors as significant contributors to family conflict and disintegration. How do we counsel families through these issues?

In the forming of a new family unit, members should be prepared to anticipate the presence of issues and be educated in ways to handle each one. Like most premarital couples, the remarrying couple believes, "We are different," "This time it will be different," or "God brought us together so we will not have the problems others had." In spite of the horrific statistics, every couple believes their story is the one with the "happily ever after" ending, ignoring the fact that only fairy tales end with happily ever after and fairy tales are not real.

"Kelly, like you, I married a wonderful man who had been married before. He brought two children into the marriage, ages five and nine. In the early months of our marriage God gave me an understanding of how important my marriage and my role as stepmother was. Jesus had a stepfather. God put a lot of confidence in stepparents when He handpicked Joseph to love, protect, and instruct His only Son. Joseph, the stepfather of Jesus, played an important role in history. Not just any man could have been a stepfather to Jesus. God is able to fill the void in families torn apart by death or divorce. Praying people are put together for God's purposes. Like Joseph, stepparents are chosen by God to minister in the family. Your goal in counseling is to change your perspective, and using the framework of remarriage issues work to reclaim your marriage in the midst of turmoil, disillusionment, negativism, attacks from other family members, and satanic assault. In the hopelessness of this setting, you can begin the journey to reclaiming love."

"Through wisdom is an house builded;
and by understanding it is established."
PROVERBS 24:3

Recommended Reading
Challenges of the Heart by Cynthia A. Miller

CHAPTER TEN

The Promotion You Didn't Want

CHALLENGES OF SINGLE PARENTING

It was not supposed to turn out this way. The wedding, the happy faces soft in the flickering candlelight, beautiful flowers, lovely bridesmaids and a handsome groom at the end of the aisle. It was a picture straight from story land—well, you were not a princess and he was not a prince or a millionaire! Other than that, it was truly destined to be "happily ever after." The road of life lie ahead as far as the eye could see without bump or bend. Then—tragedy. Shattered dreams; a broken heart; a lost companion; and you are left alone. Only not quite alone, for clinging to your skirt with tear-stained faces and hurting eyes are the children—confused and angry. What did they do wrong to make this happen? Why can't you fix it, Mommy? You always make everything better— please, please make this better!

You stand at this crossroad of life, single mom, with challenges lying before you that no one ever wants to face. It would be such a blessed relief to wake up from the horrific nightmare; unfortunately, you are not sleeping. Perhaps you could run straight into the sunset with your hair streaming in the breeze—but the little ones at your feet could not keep up. So you stand tall to fight, to survive, to maintain the family.

Where to begin? What piece do you pick up first? How can you possibly put this impossible situation back together?

Promotion

You have just been promoted—not by choice, not by desire, but by unforeseen circumstances of life. You, former vice-president, are now the president of a corporation—your family. Standing in the shadows a heavenly guide waits to help; all around is a support system—the church—to lend a hand. You will make it; your children will prosper; your family legacy will continue. Should the Lord tarry, you will see grandchildren being born again in the church and carrying on the value system that you pass down.

Trust in the Lord

The most important aspect in maintaining sanity in a world seemingly out of control is our relationship with God. The Bible is filled with promises that never fail. Those promises are ours to claim, regardless of circumstances of life.

❀ *When the future seems blotted out by the storms, it is time to cling to the Rock. The answers may not be visible, but the promises of the Word of God are.* "Trust in the LORD, and do good; so shalt thou dwell in the land, and verily thou shalt be fed. Delight thyself also in the LORD; and he shall give thee the desires of thine heart.

Commit thy way unto the LORD; trust also in him; and he shall bring it to pass" (Psalm 37:3-5).

❀ *When it is difficult to know which way to turn, God will direct.* "Trust in the LORD with all thine heart; and lean not unto thine own understanding. In all thy ways acknowledge him, and he shall direct thy paths" (Proverbs 3:5-6). "For thou art my rock and my fortress; therefore for thy name's sake lead me, and guide me" (Psalm 31:3).

❀ *When fear tries to overwhelm, the Scriptures give directive.* "The LORD is on my side; I will not fear: what can man do unto me?" (Psalm 118:6). "What time I am afraid, I will trust in thee" (Psalm 56:3).

God will be strength in weak times (II Corinthians 12:9), help in trouble (Psalm 46:1), counselor in perplexing situations (Psalm 73:24), and provision in times of need (Philippians 4:19). He will save you out of trouble (Psalm 50:15), carry your burden (Psalm 55:22), bind up your broken heart (Isaiah 61:1), deliver you from afflictions (Psalm 34:19), and give you a garment of praise for the spirit of heaviness (Isaiah 61:3).

Above all else, keep close to God. Keep the children close to God through family devotional times and faithfulness to church. With God at our side, we can face and conquer any problem or difficulty. He is the lifeline and He will never forsake us. "Let your conversation be without covetousness; and be content with such things as ye have: for he hath said, I will never leave thee, nor forsake thee" (Hebrews 13:5).

Organization Is a Must

As president of your home, it is very important to have things in order—not only the household but also schedules, responsibilities, meals, shopping, fun times, etc. Some people are organized by nature. For others, it needs to be a learned skill. There are many books available (at the library) to assist one in putting together a plan for the home. It is a must, for without organization there will be chaos, which results in frustration, words of anger, and accusation.

A simplified definition of organization is "a place for everything and everything in its place." In relationship to time, it is "a time for everything and everything in its own time." Sometimes organization appears to be rigid and confining. In actuality, it is liberating for it keeps life on track and gives one the ability to accomplish the necessities with "guilt-free" relaxation time. After all, if you "schedule" a picnic in the park, then you are responsible to stick to the schedule!

Of course, there are times when organization, scheduling, and every other form of "order" completely flies out the window. Unforeseen circumstances, sickness, accidents, or an unexpected visitor will throw one off course. Don't fret. Get through the unexpected and pick up again with your plan. The unpredictable events of life many times become treasured memories. Remember, "This too shall pass." Just roll with the punches!

The Family Is a Team

At times when a family is faced with tragedy, it is very important to regroup. Family ties are some of the strongest and most resilient bonds of our society. Even though a great loss has resulted in the family, mom and the children can close up the gap and build tight and lasting connections that will carry on to future generations. It will take some time for the wound to heal; the scar will always remain. But God is able to help mold the family vessel into a beautiful and productive piece.

It is crucial that the family views itself as a team. Mom coaches, the children are the players, and together they can be winners. True team members are not in conflict with one another but support one another. When one member is burdened, the team encourages. When one member is overwhelmed, the team pitches in to help through the crisis. When one member hurts, the team binds up the wound. When one member has a need, the team pools resources to meet the need. For instance, if one child is facing a very challenging test at school, perhaps a sibling will offer to do the nighttime chores and provide more time for study. If mom is battling a sickness "bug," the children (depending on age) may take over supper preparation and clean up. Maybe they are young, but how hard is chicken noodle soup with crackers and cheese, ice cream and Oreo cookies! Paper dinnerware and plastic spoons are easy cleanup, and mom gets a chance to rest!

As time passes and routine and order are once again established in the home, team relationship reinforces the family bonds. Children are not compared to one another but rather are encouraged to uplift each other. Every child has special abilities and talents. These gifts need to be recognized and nurtured, not only for the individual child's self-esteem but also to develop unselfishness in siblings. One may be musically talented; another may have remarkable mechanical abilities; one may be artistic; another may excel in school. Each ability is recognized, encouraged, and praised by all. No one is threatened; no one is demeaned; no one is allowed to feel worthless. Each child feels the liberty to excel in his ability and rejoice in the accomplishments of his siblings. It is family teamwork. It produces healthy family relationships and well-adjusted children.

Mom, yours is the most important task—find strengths in each of your children and help them rise to their potential. Then breed in each child the ability to rejoice when a sibling takes the limelight for a period of time. God will give you the wisdom for the task. "If any of you lack wisdom, let him ask of God, that giveth to all men liberally, and upbraideth not; and it shall be given him" (James 1:5).

The Church Is a Support System

There will certainly be days when it feels that everything is crumbling around your feet. There will be times of discouragement and borderline despair. In these times, the temptation is to withdraw from our brothers and sisters in the Lord. However, the church is the place of refuge. It is our refueling station. The weary and discouraged soul is refreshed in the house of the Lord. "It will be a shelter and shade from the heat of the day, and a refuge and hiding place from the storm and rain" (Isaiah 4:6, NIV). We are mandated in the Bible to be faithful to church: "Not forsaking the assembling of ourselves together, as the manner of some is; but exhorting one another: and so much the more, as ye see the day approaching" (Hebrews 10:25).

The children need the stability of regular church attendance. There will be church functions geared especially for them that will help build their social skills and will give them a sense of belonging. Children love routine, especially little children. They love tradition. They will look forward to the annual Sunday school picnic, the Christmas program, children's church, and Sunday school.

The absence of dad in the home removes the male influence. Many times a grandpa or uncle can help fill this gap. If there are no male relatives living close, a godly man of the church can mentor a young boy in his growing up years. Many churches have a Boy Scout program which is a very exciting and educational experience for a young boy. Around the age of twelve years, a young man intensely desires to be involved in "man" things like fishing, hunting, and camping out. It may scare mom to death, but if he is in a godly and healthy atmosphere, let him go.

The pastor and his wife will assist in major decisions that you face. They are concerned for the well-being of your entire family and will offer good counsel. You pastor watches for your soul and the souls of your children. God gives him special wisdom for each member of the congregation, and he will help guide your steps if you seek his counsel.

Stay close to the church, even if your tendency is to distance yourself because people are uneasy with your status. You need the fellowship of the family of God.

Coping with Loneliness

Very likely loneliness will bubble to the top of the pile of difficulties facing a single parent, especially if singleness hits suddenly through death or divorce. In helping to deal with this problem, it is crucial that one keeps her sense of self-worth. Always keep in mind that you are a child of God; that He holds you in His hand; that He knew you in the womb; that He has specific plan for your life. You are priceless in the sight of God; you are worth more than the entire world. Even though God is not always responsible for what happens in our lives, for the will of man factors into situations, He is never surprised. He is able to pick up broken pieces and remake them into a beautiful vessel.

When you view yourself in the mirror each morning, remember you are a daughter of the king; you are precious in His sight. No one can take that away from you. Part of the process of building your self-esteem is forgiveness. Perhaps you will need to forgive yourself; perhaps you will need to forgive another human being. Release yourself from the guilt of an unforgiving spirit that can only develop a root of bitterness in your heart to your own destruction. Set yourself free to become what God has purposed.

Another aspect in the battle against loneliness is a sense of belonging. Of course, you belong to your family. You are vital to the future of your children. You also belong to the church and are a very important part of the body of believers. There may be areas of involvement that are impossible because of added responsibilities at home. However, plunge into everything that is possible and practical. You will enjoy the sense of belonging and affirmation that accompanies being a blessing to others!

Then There Are the Finances!

One of the major challenges facing you is finances. Chances are good that there has been a great change in the financial structure of your home. The already limited income has suddenly become more limited. Perhaps working is not merely a choice now but a necessity. Financial problems can create tremendous stress to the home. It may be necessary to downsize to economize. The children can become a part of helping make the decisions to cope with the family budget. Include God in your decision process. He has an unfailing financial program that works in every situation. When we follow God's financial plan, we claim God's financial promises! "I have been young, and now am old; yet have I not seen the righteous forsaken, nor his seed begging bread" (Psalm 37:25). "Bring ye all the tithes into the storehouse, that there may be meat in mine house, and prove me now herewith, saith the LORD of hosts, if I will not open you the windows of heaven, and pour you out a blessing, that there shall not be room enough to receive it" (Malachi 3:10).

Connected with finances, of course, is your choice of job. One area of concern is "latchkey" children. It may be very difficult to arrange your working schedule to accommodate the children's school schedule. It is best to avoid your children coming home to an empty house. Extended family members could possibly help in this eventuality, or a trusted church family.

In making financial and job choice decisions, remember to seek godly counsel. Another perspective, an additional source for ideas and suggestions, will help you make the right choices.

A Little Time for You

It is a must to plan fun times—for yourself and for your family. You may not have extra finances to accommodate this, but there are economic ways to have lots of fun. On holidays and vacations, take time for rest and relaxation. If you live close to a park, a picnic is always in order. Generally there is equipment for the children's enjoyment. The fresh air, the sound of birds, and the rustling of leaves in the treetops envelopes one's being and helps work out the tension. Even a backyard picnic is lots of fun—especially if the children are small and have access to a splash pool. Water and sand never lose their magic in the "favorite things" a child enjoys.

Family vacations become favored memories. If you ever listen to adults reminiscing, many times they will tell of family vacation times. It may require innovative thinking, but you can plan a fun vacation without breaking the family's financial bank. Staying at home and visiting interesting sites in your city, tenting in the back yard, spreading the sleeping bags in the family room and reading by flashlight—the list is endless. Does your church district have a campground? Ever tent with the children for family camp? Hot? Probably. Work? Very likely. Memories? Definitely!

Holidays get you down? Plan to invite someone over. Another lady's help in the kitchen is always appreciated! Share the menu, share the work, and build an unforgettable memory. You might even start a tradition!

Ever play monopoly for a week? Continue the game for the whole vacation! Bail out the bankrupt players and keep it going! Or attempt a big puzzle—keep it spread out for the entire holiday period. Everyone will rejoice to "find" a few lost pieces!

Then there are times when you, mom, need a little reprieve just for yourself. Pamper yourself occasionally. Can't afford the babysitter? Try barter babysitting with someone from the church. Perhaps a young couple would welcome exchange babysitting. They can't afford the babysitter either, but long for a night out. Your children may be older and would enjoy an evening to entertain and care for an infant.

Whatever it takes to make it happen, plan times of relaxation for yourself and the children. Let them be a part of the planning process. Sometimes anticipation is actually better than realization—the excitement of planning . . . counting the days until. These will be cherished times!

To Marry or Not to Marry!

It is a normal desire to have the family "complete" once again. A mother wants to "fix" the situation. Not only for herself but also for the well-being of the children. It may be very difficult to blend families or add a stepfather to your family unit. A single-mom home that is filled with unity, love and contentment—even though small and lacking extras—is much more healthy for the children than a house with a stepfather who may be cruel, controlling, and abusive. Some men find it difficult to accept and love children who are not their biological offspring.

If a possible marriage opportunity surfaces, follow some precautionary procedures:

1. Remember you are vulnerable, so seek godly counsel *before* you fall in love.

2. Take careful note of how your male friend interacts with your children. If there are tensions before marriage, if there are troubling relationship indications, beware! Walking down an aisle will not sprinkle the situation with a magic solution. Things will very likely deteriorate after the marriage!

3. It is tough for children to submit to the discipline of an adult who they may feel is intruding into their family. It may take a period of time before the children accept a stepfather as an authority figure. He must win their respect and confidence. If you are not well on the road to acceptance before the marriage, it is a good indication that acceptance may never materialize.

4. Your sons may feel protective of you and resent "another man" entering what they consider their area of responsibility. It may take a lot of love and patience to convince your sons that they can trust their mother to the care of this "trespasser" on their territory!

Let life happen. Do not continually reach for the illusive dream and fret when it cannot be attained. Do not try to make marriage happen; do not worry if it does not happen. Enjoy the journey. Seize the precious moments of everyday living that blend together to make memories.

You Will Survive!

Many women have walked the path before you. They have lived fulfilled lives and raised wonderful children who are productive in society in every area of life—missionaries, ministers, doctors, teachers—the list is long and prestigious. You, too, will someday look back to a treasure house of memories. Some will be of good times;

some will be of tough times. But even memory of the tough times will bring a sense of accomplishment. You survived! You made it! You, and the kids—with God and the church!

CHAPTER ELEVEN

Alone in a Crowd

MAKING LONELINESS MY FRIEND

It felt like 120° F, and my heart was pounding like a drum as I stepped off the plane onto the soil of Africa for the first time. My eyes felt stretched as I searched frantically for a familiar face or a cardboard sign with my name on it. Finding neither, I began the long slow walk through customs and immigration that would finally admit me to the land I had prayed for, dreamed about, and desperately tried to reach for so long. I spoke slowly and carefully to everyone. My ears strained to catch the unfamiliar English. I stood in line with the other aliens in this capital city and continued my search for someone— anyone who was looking for me.

It was no use. No one had met me.

When all formalities had been completed, I kept my eyes alert as bags rolled off the ramp. There it was— my luggage! Then the challenge—how to manhandle both pieces of luggage onto a cart and keep a little man (about as tall as my shoulder) from taking it away from me. The missionary had told me to "act like you know what you are doing." I put on such a great show that I should have received an Oscar!

What next? Nothing prepared me for the sea of faces that met me outside the lobby's mechanical doors. It was total chaos. Everyone wanted to be my taxi driver or take my luggage or help me in some way. I "acted" like I knew exactly where I was going, chose one person, and elbowed the others out of my way—literally.

I wish I could describe the total terror I felt as a 24-year-old single girl from a small town in south Alabama. I got into the back seat of a taxi and told the driver, "Domestic airport, please."

He asked which flight I was taking; when I told him, he informed me that I would never make it.

I insisted, so away we went down roads that should never have been called roads, through traffic that should never have been allowed! The only lights were flickering candles made from tin cans containing a little oil and a homemade wick.

He may have been a reckless driver, but my taxi driver knew his flights. As we pulled into the domestic airport area my flight was taking off into the night air. My heart sank right through my toes, but I was acting like I knew what I was doing. I told the taxi driver to take me back to the international airport.

He offered the names of various hotels in the city, but I knew my meager funds would not survive a visit to any of them. Thank God, he did as I asked and took me straight to the place from which he had earlier brought me. He could have been motivated by the fact that I had not yet paid him. I had not exchanged my money.

With my luggage back inside the airport and the taxi driver paid, I looked for a restroom. I had never before encountered a restroom like the one I entered.

On this night in July 1981, I was alone in a city of about ten million people, and no one knew I was there! The missionary lived a good two-day drive or one-hour plane ride plus a three-hour drive away. I couldn't call him; he didn't have a phone. I could not call my parents; I did not have enough money, and the airport did not allow collect calls. I was stuck here. I was afraid, and I was alone.

Alone in a Crowd

Have you ever been in a sea of people, yet felt alone? You probably were not in a foreign country, but you might as well have been. Feeling alone does not require that you be by yourself. What does it mean to feel lonely? Picture this:

- ❀ You are in a large city of strangers with not one friend and no money to call home. Maybe you are a home missionary's wife and have just moved to a place far from everyone you know and love.
- ❀ You are the only "youth" in the youth group of your local church.
- ❀ On a large university campus you are the only person who has obeyed the gospel—at least you do not know that anyone else on campus has obeyed the gospel.
- ❀ There is no church in the city where you live and work; for fellowship you have to drive at least an hour each way every weekend.
- ❀ You arrive alone for family get-togethers and holidays, and you leave alone—single, but with a great career.

❧ You stand in front of a room full of women who are looking to you for direction and guidance; you ask yourself, "Is there anyone here to whom I can talk or who will understand me?"

❧ You are far from home when word comes of the death of a loved one. You cannot possibly go to the funeral and therefore say good-bye from a distance.

❧ Your spouse of many years dies. In an instant you change from being a pastor's wife to being a saint in the local church.

❧ Your health fails. You are forced to leave your home and live in a nursing home or a retirement center so that you can have medical attention at all times.

Do any of these scenarios trigger the phrase "been there, done that" in your brain? Much of life is spent surrounded by people, yet you may at times feel alone. It is a natural feeling, experienced most when surrounded by those who seem to have everything we desire. It would probably amaze us to know that those with everything going for them also feel lonely. It will help if you realize that loneliness is often just that—a feeling. Somewhere else in the world, somebody is feeling this same type of loneliness.

How Can We Deal with Loneliness?

A favorite verse of Scripture says: "And we know that all things work together for good to them that love God, to them who are the called according to his purpose" (Romans 8:28).

You may not feel like things are working for good when the loneliness is so strong that you can barely breathe. Nevertheless, this verse is true. God can use our loneliness to turn us toward Him.

"Loneliness becomes our 'friend' when it forces us to enjoy the friendship of God as much as we would the friendship of others."
—BILL GOTHARD

Our best source of help comes from the Word of God. When you are lonely, you may not want to sit and read the Bible. You probably want a friend to be with you. But the Bible is your friend; it is the word of someone who will never leave you or forsake you (Hebrews 13:5). While you are feeling lonely, that Friend, Jesus, is already there, waiting for you to talk to Him. God's Word (His talk to us) has many examples of people who were lonely. These examples can help us understand some of the things that cause loneliness.

The psalmist David understood what it meant to feel lonely. His life was an emotional roller coaster. He was anointed to be the king of Israel, but he still took care of the sheep. He killed a giant, after which he went home to his father's house. He played his harp for the king; he was then sent back home while his brothers left to fight a war. He was brought to the palace and married to the king's daughter, but soon he was driven from the palace by his father-in-law and became a fugitive, living in caves with the vagabonds of society for companions. Loneliness? Yes, David experienced loneliness. He wrote: "Reproach hath broken my heart; and I am full of heaviness: and I looked for some to take pity, but there was none; and for comforters, but I found none" (Psalm 69:20).

When you are feeling lonely, read from the Book of Psalms. You will find that David felt many of your same emotions.

Ruth understood loneliness. Widowed at an early age, she chose to follow her mother-in-law into a strange country. Ruth faced prejudice and the loneliness of being different. She committed her life in loyalty to her dead husband's mother and her God. Her determination to follow God and live according to His laws, no matter what, won her a place in the lineage of Jesus Christ (Matthew 1:5).

Ruth's loneliness was turned to joy because she chose to make Naomi's God her God. With a sincere pledge to her mother-in-law, Ruth began her journey from sorrow to a new life. Her words to Naomi reveal her faith and loyalty: "Entreat me not to leave you, or to turn back from following after you; for wherever you go, I will go; and wherever you lodge, I will lodge; your people shall be my people, and your God, my God. Where you die, I will die, and there will I be buried. The LORD do so to me, and more also, if anything but death parts you and me" (Ruth 1:16-17, NKJV).

These verses have been repeated many times in wedding ceremony vows. They are also true of our determination to follow God's will, wherever it leads. Do not let anything stop you from knowing God for yourself.

Jesus was a frequent visitor in the home of two sisters and their brother. He loved them all (John 11:5). However, they reacted to His nearness in different ways. Martha was the practical one, always busy and taking care of the Master. Mary was the one found at His feet, listening to His words (Luke 10:38-42).

When Lazarus got sick, they sent word to Jesus because they knew of His healing power. Mary and Martha were single women and depended heavily on their brother. When he died, they suffered severe loss and loneliness (John 11:17-19).

When Jesus came, Martha immediately went out to meet Him. Little did she know that the glory of God was about to be revealed to them. At Jesus' three short words, their brother Lazarus was restored to life. Mary and Martha's loneliness lasted only four days. Many times, we feel as though the loneliness will never end, but it will.

The interesting thing about these sisters is their response to God's deliverance and grace. John 12 tells about Jesus' visit to their house after Lazarus' resurrection. Martha still served. Lazarus sat at the table with Jesus. Mary took her place at Jesus' feet.

This time, Mary brought costly ointment, anointed Jesus' feet, and wiped His feet with her hair. The ointment was especially precious, but Mary understood that her most valuable possession was best spent at the feet of Jesus, as was her life. She understood that Jesus was the answer to her loneliness. Her devotion and sacrifice built a memorial in her name (Matthew 26:13).

The Way Out

The best way to overcome loneliness is to pour ourselves into service, devotion, and sacrifice for Jesus. We are working not only for Him as Martha did, but also we are ministering to Him as Mary did. This is the highest purpose for our lives, a personal heartfelt love and devotion to Jesus that expresses itself in our love and service to others.

"I beseech you therefore, brethren, by the mercies of God, that ye present your bodies a living sacrifice, holy, acceptable unto God, which is your reasonable service. And be not conformed to this world: but be ye transformed by the renewing of your mind, that ye may prove what is that good, and acceptable, and perfect, will of God" (Romans 12:1-2).

Obedience to Paul's admonition can erase loneliness. When I present my body for God's service, I look for ways to be used in His kingdom. I spend time in the

Word, listening to God's voice. I seek relationships with others to be able to share the good news of salvation. I show others God's love and sacrifice by my works. I move outside of my isolation, always seeking those Jesus would have me to reach. I no longer have time to be lonely. No matter where this sacrifice leads me, God is always there, helping me and sharing the load. Loneliness has no place in my life. My transformed mind feeds on the good things of God.

"Wherefore do ye spend money for that which is not bread? and your labour for that which satisfieth not? hearken diligently unto me, and eat ye that which is good, and let your soul delight itself in fatness" (Isaiah 55:2).

No matter what your work—teacher, construction worker, doctor, lawyer, housewife, or garbage collector—do it heartily "as unto the Lord," putting God's kingdom first.

A large portion of Jesus' famous Sermon on the Mount encourages us not to worry about the practical things of life, even our loneliness: "But seek ye first the kingdom of God, and his righteousness; and all these things shall be added unto you" (Matthew 6:33).

Seek (actively search for) God first, and He will remove your loneliness.

It was four days after I turned twenty-nine years old when I walked down the aisle on my father's arm. Three years before in that crowded, lonely airport, I did not dream that in that foreign land I would meet and work with a young man dedicated to missions. I had not planned to find God's will with a husband. I just wanted God's will, whatever it was and wherever it took me. God gave me the desires of my heart (even some I never spoke aloud).

I now serve God on the mission field with a husband dedicated to the work of the Lord—a husband who always seeks God's will before making a decision and is the spiritual leader for our family. God's will for my life was more than I ever asked or even imagined. It was worth every lonely day.

Loneliness proved to be my friend by pushing me to my knees, into the Word, and ever closer to Jesus, my best friend.

CHAPTER TWELVE

Healing for Extreme Hurts

FINDING PEACE WHEN RELATIONSHIPS SHATTER

What a disappointment when we realize that the perfect life we envisioned is not the reality of life we experience. Are you suffering from extreme emotional pain because of a breakup in marriage? Has your child left home, leaving a gapping hole with lacerations of dashed hopes of restoring the relationship between you? Are you hurting from a friendship that ended in ugly words and irreparable damage? Are you experiencing the set-back of a jilted love?

Divorce Damage

Stumbling through the front door, her face distorted with pain, she fell sobbing into the arms of her mother. A river of tears left her eyes swollen, and red blotchy patches appeared upon her wet cheeks and neck. What could have caused such suffering?

I was sitting in the living room of my parent's home when my beloved sister broke the heartsick news: "He

131

kicked me out. He doesn't want me anymore!" I flew from my chair and threw my arms around my sister. I knew she was talking about her husband of seven years. The vindictive climax of their turbulent relationship had finally come to a head. My sweet little sister was being thrown out—not only out of her home, but thrown out of her husband's life, a relationship she worked for seven years to hold together. I could not imagine how she could continue loving this guy, but that love kept her going back, even after he threw her out one, two, and now three times.

I was convinced the love of our family would make it all better. I believed we were all she would need for support during this time of devastation. I was determined to love her back to emotional health, convinced that though it would not be easy to fill the place her husband vacated, neither was it impossible. How little did I know.

I kept close tabs on my sister, calling her often and letting her talk whenever she wanted to. After several months, I realized there was a void I could not fill. There was a hurt I could not heal, and there was damage that I could not make right. I experienced a helplessness I could not express. How could I make up for all the damage? My sister's rehabilitation would have to come from somewhere other than me; something deeper than my love would have to penetrate the scars that told the story of how deep the wounds.

Parting Pain in Parenthood

Matthew slammed the door and stormed from the house. Harsh words still stung in Megan's ears as she watched her precious firstborn stalk across the driveway, mount his motorcycle and peel out, leaving a trail of exhaust smoke that reminded her of the stormy past few months. Where did she go wrong? How did it come to this? With a hopeless sigh, she flopped on the couch to do some serious soul-searching between sobs. The truth is, this paramount problem did not begin today. No, it had been coming for a long time. It just came to a climax today. Now all Megan could feel was a cold chill of hopelessness that draped over her heart like a shroud.

Jilted and Joyless

Karen walked into my office and I immediately knew there was something wrong. Her shoulders sagged, her eyes were swollen and red from crying, and that cheerful, upturned smile had disappeared from her young innocent face. "What's the matter?" I asked rising from my place behind the large cherry-wood desk. Rejection was written all over her. She cried in my arms for a few minutes and then began to tell me her story.

Life had been wonderful. This guy she was seeing was perfect! He loved God, he loved her, and it sounded like there might be wedding bells in the near future! Then suddenly, the world came crashing down around her. Mr. Wonderful felt in the Holy Ghost to break up. Karen was devastated! What could I say? I silently prayed and asked God for guidance.

The common denominator between my sister, Megan, and Karen is the unfortunate experience of shattered relationships. Does it hurt? Of course it hurts; and at the onset, it feels like the emotional pain will never go away.

I presume since you are reading this chapter, you are either hurting and in need of healing, or someone you love is hurting and you are looking for answers. I cannot promise that the pain will go away today. But I can tell you that tomorrow the sun will rise, the birds will sing, and, as hard as it may be to imagine, life will go on. Life may not acknowledge your pain, but time will. Time uses the advantage of fading memories to heal the most excruciating hurts. But time will not be rushed, nor will the sun refuse to shine.

As you probably already know, emotional pain is real. It is as real as a cut on your arm, or a knife plunged into your heart. Emotional pain, like physical pain, has to have time to heal.

Regardless of how long you have allowed yourself to love someone, when it is ripped away, the outcome is to some degree the same. To a mother whose child has just walked out of her life, to a wife whose husband never came home, or two friends angrily parting ways, losing the relationship of someone you loved is devastating.

You have spent precious time cultivating a relationship, cautiously moving into a vulnerable world. You took the gamble of losing yourself in someone else. Sharing your dreams, plans, and secrets leaves you feeling exposed, but at the time you felt the gamble was worth it. When you are hurt, it is tempting to close the door on your heart and never let anyone else come in. But if you never take the chance, you will never experience love again. Loving is always worth it because you learn from loving. You learn from someone you have loved and your person expands because of the knowledge you gain in having loved. Even if love is not reciprocated, you have done the other person a great favor by imparting Jesus Christ to them. God is love and when we love, we give others God. When love is returned, the past pain and heartache is soon forgotten or at least fades with time.

The Time Factor

Compare losing a loved one relationally with losing someone to death. Emotionally, you have to grieve the loss, just as the body has to adjust to amputation or a body-part removal. No matter how small the body part, adjustment is necessary for natural rehabilitation. The same is true with emotional injury. No matter how long the relationship has been alive, adjustment is necessary for natural rehabilitation. For all healing, natural or emotional, time is of the essence.

Time, that four letter word, seldom seems to be on our side. It snails along when we are in pain and moves too rapidly when we are laughing and life is wonderful. You have heard, "time flies when you're having fun," but the flip side is that time crawls at a snail's pace when we are hurting.

Aside from time, you may be asking what other things help heal pain. There are certain steps in the healing process. Relationship loss comes in many different ways. Death, divorce, estrangement, severed friendships, miscarriage, and other relational losses are just a few examples. The common thread that weaves itself throughout every loss is grief. Much like death, you have to grieve the loss of a loved one even though he or she is still living.

The Place Healing Begins

Many years after the pain of her divorce was healed, my sister said, "I finally found healing when I moved closer to God." Healing finally begins when we allow God to administer the antiseptic of His blood. Isaiah 53:5 says, "But He was wounded for our transgressions, He was bruised for our iniquities; the chastisement for our peace was upon Him, and by His stripes we are healed" (NKJV).

Family and friends may serve as a support group, but when you fall on your knees and talk to God, you are talking to the only Friend that can change the situation.

The Anger and Blame Game

The phases of emotional trauma are feeling hurt, and experiencing low self-esteem. Phrases like, "I'm broken; I'm shattered, I'm worthless; It's all my fault, I'm lonely,

I'm afraid and I'm confused" pass through your mind unbridled. Then comes anger which carries the blame game on piggyback. You are angry with the one who hurt you; you are angry with yourself for various reasons. Perhaps you are angry because you did not see the break-up coming, angry with the way you handled escalated situations with your teenage child, or angry because of lost verbal combats with a friend. You may be angry just because you feel you were innocent and were wrongly treated; angry because you were abused, emotionally, physically, and/or psychologically.

You may feel that you have a right to be angry. Then, to justify your anger, you must blame someone, anyone. It may start with the other person in the relationship—your ex-husband, friend, fiancé or someone involved in the larger picture. It may be easier to blame yourself, or God, because you can vent your feelings here and now. If you blame yourself, low self-esteem is inevitable. God knows how you feel. He has experienced the rejection of a spurned lover. Hosea is an excellent book to read about God's love for Israel and how Israel spurned His affection.

So here you are, facing the carousal of pain again. At first you move from one phase to the other very slowly or you may vacillate between them. If you want to move on, there are steps that must be taken emotionally to graduate from each phase, never to return. This is the first step in finding the road to recovery and emotional rehabilitation.

It Is Okay to Cry

Emotional pain needs an outlet. When you feel the pain, it helps to cry. Crying is a natural release of emotion. If you feel like crying now, take a moment to cry. Cry about the love you have lost. Cry about the hurt that you feel or you caused. Cry because you know things could have been different. Go ahead and cry. Every day may seem like a bad day at first and you may cry a lot. But hold on; they will get farther apart. Your bouts of crying and depression will begin to separate themselves from each other. Gradually, you will notice a good day springing up once in a while. Those good days will get closer together with time.

Once you have cried, it is time to move on. Crying helps you feel better temporarily, but you do not want to live here. Crying helps, but it will not heal you exclusively.

Many times when you are hurting, you lash out in anger. If you are feeling angry, express it. If you cannot express why you are angry toward someone, drop it. The anger may be there but directed toward the wrong person. Evaluate the source of your feelings when you are alone to see with whom you are actually angry. Tell someone how you are feeling. Find someone who is non-related to the situation and willing to listen. A pastor, pastor's wife, friend, or mentor may be helpful.

Many people experience anger toward God. It is easy to raise a fist at Him, because it seems safe; He will not hit you or yell at you or reject you. If your anger is directed toward God, express it. You must admit you are angry and let Him know. At least it keeps the communication open. If you clam up, the communication is lost. Keep the communication open with God, even if it is anger. He understands and will help you to understand in time. Just do not cut him off!

Moving On to Forgiveness

Anger usually brings you to the "placing blame" stage. Once you realize you are angry at someone for a good reason, blame sets in. You feel like all this happened because of "him," or "it's all her fault!" More times than not, you will probably blame yourself. At this point you must make yourself move to the "forgiveness" stage. Ask

God to help you with this. Start with God; ask God to forgive you and help you learn to forgive yourself. After you have asked for help in forgiving God and yourself, ask Him to help you forgive others you feel are partially responsible for your demise. When you forgive those who have wronged you, peace will be released and you will begin to feel freedom from pain. You will be free at last to embrace peace; smile again, and move on with life!

Review what to do with emotional pain:

- ❀ Hurt – When you feel hurt, find an outlet.
- ❀ Low self-esteem – Allow God to love you and re-affirm who you are.
- ❀ Anger – Express your anger and move on.
- ❀ Blame – Learn to forgive those responsible.

Trust that God knows your future. If you have been faithful to Him, He will guide the events in your life, directing you in His path. Whatever your circumstance, realize that God knows right where you are. Yes, He knows. He knows it all—every fearful night; every swing that is dodged. He knows every anxious moment waiting for the phone to ring; every ounce of rejection that flows in your veins. Yes, He knows it all. And He wants to comfort you and heal you today.

> *"Casting all your care upon him;*
> *for he careth for you."*
> I Peter 5:7

CHAPTER THIRTEEN

I'm Not Perfect . . . Just Forgiven

MODELING GOD'S FORGIVENESS

Jesus Christ was the only person in the history of humanity who did not need forgiveness (Romans 3:10, 23; II Corinthians 5:21). All others did need it, do need it, and will need it because we are all imperfect.

The success of all relationships, whether with divinity or humanity, hinges on forgiveness. When our relationship with God flourishes, so do our relationships with others. When our relationships with others suffer, so does our relationship with God. (See John 15:9-12; I Peter 3:7; I John 4:20-21.) All sin, including sin against another person, is against God (cp. Psalm 51:4).[i]

Jesus taught His disciples: "It is impossible but that offences will come" (Luke 17:1). The only way to avoid being hurt sometime is to avoid all possibility of love, because to risk love is to risk hurt. Loving others requires that we be willing to forgive them; forgiving others requires that we be willing to love them.

Forgiveness plays an integral role in our salvation—we need divine forgiveness, we need to forgive others, and we need to receive the forgiveness of others.

Forgiveness is a key to the success of all relationships. Exactly what is forgiveness? The misconceptions of secular humanists, psychotherapists, and some Christian counselors have crept into the church, distorting its meaning. Consequently, many of us blunder through a maze of bruised, wounded, or severed relationships, wondering why it takes so long for them to heal. First, let us establish what forgiveness is not.

Forgiveness Is Not . . .

1. *Excusing.* Modern psychology has altered the concept of sin, changing the label to sickness. It attributes unacceptable or destructive behavior to emotional or other problems, which in turn transforms offenders into victims and frees them from all personal responsibility for their actions. When sin is redefined and excused, the person who was wronged is left without recourse. Worse, wrongdoers are left in their sin and guilt, unforgiven, with all the dire consequences that arise from unforgiven sin.[ii]

2. *Apology.* Karen's teenage son, Sean, works for a fellow church member. While helping to repair the air conditioner in the home of another church member, Sean sees a box of new checks on the desk and furtively takes a pack. Later, the church member angrily confronts Karen because she has discovered that it was Sean who forged several checks worth hundreds of dollars. Shocked and mortified, Karen confronts Sean. When Sean defensively says, "I'm sorry, okay?" he has not asked for forgiveness; he has not even admitted to wrongdoing. Mere apologies lack confession and repentance, without which forgiveness cannot occur. Sean's behavior probably will not change unless he comes to a place of confession and repentance.

3. *Minimizing the wrong or the hurt.* The honey-moon is over. John is totally involved with job and ministry. Sarah, who is eight months pregnant, longs for the attention, tender moments, and the sweet nothings that John lavished on her when they dated. At dinner with relatives, the subject turns to romance, and Sarah blurts, "I wish we still had a little romance in our marriage." John looks pointedly at her belly and bellows, "Oh, *you* sure look like *you* haven't been having any romance!" Everyone laughs, but Sarah is crushed. On the way home she tells John that he has hurt her feelings. He heaves a sigh and rolls his eyes. "You're too sensitive," he accuses. "I'm tired of treating you with kid gloves." Not only has John justified his offense, he has also minimized Sarah's hurt by criticizing her reaction. Because nothing is resolved, John will probably continue to trample on Sarah's feelings. Their relationship is stymied until they can learn how to give and receive forgiveness.

4. *Healing memories.* Felicia suffers with anorexia. She reveals to a Christian counselor that when she and her sister were young, the man they thought was their dad railed at them every night, making dinner an ordeal: "Look at you fatsoes stuffing your faces. Pigs! No man will ever want you slobs!" They always left the table in tears. They did not find out until they were adults that the man was actually their stepfather. The counselor encourages Felicia to mentally relive the unpleasant events, while visualizing Jesus beside her, assuring her that His healing presence will cause all bad effects (such as anorexia) to vanish. This technique is unbiblical in that it misrepresents Jesus and bypasses the biblical principles of forgiveness.[iii]

Discovering Biblical Forgiveness

"Be ye kind one to another, tenderhearted, forgiving one another, even as God for Christ's sake hath forgiven you" (Ephesians 4:32). We should model our forgiveness of others after the manner in which God forgives us. God does not forgive us because we deserve it. He forgives because He loves us (Ephesians 2:4-6; I John 4:8-10).[iv]

The Old Testament word for "forgive" means "to remit a debt or to pay it." We release someone from the guilt or penalty of (sin) or to cancel or refrain from inflicting (the penalty). Paul says that the Lord "blot[s] out the handwriting of ordinances . . . against us . . . nailing it to his cross" (Colossians 2:14). "I, even I, am he that blot[s] out thy transgressions for mine own sake, and will not remember [your] sins" (Isaiah 43:25; cp. Jeremiah 31:34b).

Not one of us can pay the immense debt we owe for our sin. Although He does not remove all consequences for our sin, God forgives us for His own sake because He wants us to be reconciled to Him. And He will not come back later and use it against us.[v]

The fact that God has forgiven our debt makes reconciliation with Him possible (II Corinthians 5:19; Hebrews 2:17). Our initial experience of spiritual birth and reconciliation is through our faith in Him and our obedience to Acts 2:38, which includes repentance. When we need forgiveness after that, He still requires confession and repentance (Romans 2:4; II Peter 3:9; I John 1:9).

Following the Forgiveness Model

Forgiveness is a divine attribute. When we have the Holy Spirit and we are abiding in the vine (John 15:5), we can forgive as God does (Colossians 3:12-13; I Peter 2:21-23).[vi] In Luke 17:3 and Matthew 18:15, Jesus provides a forgiveness template: "If thy brother trespass against thee, rebuke him [tell him his fault between thee and him alone]; and if he repent, forgive him." This pattern parallels God's forgiveness toward us:

1. The offender may not deserve our forgiveness; we do it because we want him to be reconciled to us. If we do not have the heart to forgive, we must pray in order to tap into the Holy Spirit's willingness to forgive (Luke 6:27-37).

2. Confession means acknowledging wrongdoing and taking responsibility for it. Repentance is changing one's mind and consequently one's behavior (James 5:16; Colossians 3:12-14). Repentance is necessary so that the offender will not continue the hurtful behavior.

3. If the offender sincerely confesses and repents, then, according to God's Word, we are obligated to forgive. This means we cancel the debt with no penalty to the offender and that we will not use it against him later (Romans 12:17-21).

4. It is impossible to forget the offense, but we must *choose not to remember.* Thankfully, in the course of time we actually do forget the offense!

5. Confrontation, confession, repentance, and forgiveness finally bring us to the ultimate goal of the process: reconciliation. If we are successful, the relationship can be healed.

Using the Forgiveness Model

You are probably thinking: "If it takes that much effort to straighten out every conflict, I won't have a life." Peter must have been just as perplexed after he asked Jesus, "Lord, how oft shall my brother sin against me, and I forgive him?" (Matthew 18:21-22). Peter eventually learned about forgiveness and wrote: "Above all things have fervent charity among yourselves: for charity shall cover the multitude of sins" (I Peter 4:8). Every incident is not worth the emotional fuel it burns. We should learn to let our love for God and one another cover it and simply let it go.

Any incident that is serious enough to bruise, wound, or sever a relationship needs reconciliation. The biblical way to bring it about is to follow the pattern given in Luke 17:3 and Matthew 18:15.

Janette and Alicia are good friends whose husbands pastor churches in neighboring towns. Janette teaches in their church's Christian school. Janette and Gavin's youngest child is Hannah. Alicia and Rex (oldest) are raising their granddaughter, Candy.

When Rex's congregation dwindles to three members, Gavin sympathetically invites them to join his congregation. Alicia and Rex accept the offer and move to Gavin and Alicia's town. They enroll Candy in the Christian school.

Candy and Hannah are both in Janette's class. Candy is cute and talkative while Hannah is quiet and bookish. At first the girls are inseparable. Then the good times hit a snag. After school every day, Candy reports to "Nanny" that Hannah is talking about her to other girls and picking on her on the playground. Candy continues this day after day, until Alicia becomes very upset. Instead of calling Janette to verify Candy's stories, Alicia scorches the phone lines to other parents, complaining that Hannah is a bully and that Janette is an unfair teacher. One of the parents finally tells Janette about the turmoil.

Janette is so hurt by her friend's accusations that she does not know what to do. She asks Hannah if the stories are true. They discuss the incidents and Janette realizes that Candy is cleverly twisting events to make them appear like persecution. Then she can manipulate Nanny and enjoy the furor.

Janette hesitates to confront Alicia. She explains to Hannah that Candy may be acting out of jealousy because Hannah is the pastor's daughter and Candy no longer enjoys a similar status. She tells Hannah to stay away from Candy, but the stories and the furor continue.

It's time for the annual ladies' retreat, during which Janette and Alicia have always shared a room. Janette feels that God wants her to ask Alicia to share a room with her again this year. When she does, Alicia begins to cry. "I thought you would never want to room with me or ever again have anything to do with me."

"Alicia, I do want to room with you because I still love you. And I want us to remain friends." Alicia repents and Janette forgives her. Alicia also confesses her wrong to the ones she has called, and they forgive her. Alicia promises Janette that she will correct Candy's behavior.

The Case of the Unrepentant Offender

What happens if we lovingly confront an offender, but she will not confess and repent? Jesus covers this in Matthew 18:16-17. These two verses reinforce the belief that forgiveness is conditional. They also invalidate the teaching that we must forgive others no matter how they respond. God did not design the forgiveness model as a therapeutic "feel good" technique for the one doing the forgiving. God is interested in *reconciliation*, which is brought about by *repentance*.

It is wrong to automatically assume that the one who withholds forgiveness is the one who is to blame for the problem in a relationship. That is true only if the offender has already shown evidence of repentance, but the offended party chooses not to forgive.

Consequences for Those Who Refuse to Forgive

Read the parable of the unforgiving servant (Matthew 18:23-35).

Unforgiveness is a choice. When a person chooses not to forgive a person who has wronged her and then repented, she becomes susceptible to many spiritual ills: bitterness, anger, strife, evil speaking, malice, revenge

(Romans 12:19; Ephesians 4:31; Hebrews 12:15). An unforgiving spirit is actually a form of hatred.[vii] How can you know if you have an unforgiving spirit?

❀ Do you keep rehearsing the painful memory of a hurt done to you?

❀ Can you honestly wish the offending person well?

❀ Do you want the offending person to feel pain, suffering, and hurt to the degree you believe you have felt them?[viii]

What the unforgiving person does not realize is that she causes herself more harm than the offender has caused. She keeps unforgiveness bottled up inside until it sours into bitterness and resentment. She becomes trapped in emotional bondage, tormented with memories and impaired with a diminished capacity to love. Intimacy becomes difficult; relationships escalate into anger and fighting. Her relationship with God becomes uneasy and restless. She may seek retaliation. Her physical body suffers from an overloaded nervous system and long-standing stress.[ix]

The person who has developed an unforgiving spirit is in an unpardonable state—God cannot and will not forgive her (Matthew 6:12, 14-15). God refuses to listen to her prayers because she stubbornly refuses to forgive the one who offended her. God will permit her to be destroyed by her own sin if she so desires (Galatians 6:7-8). Hopefully, loss of the blessings of fellowship with God and the ruined relationships with others may cause her to come to her senses (as did the prodigal son).

God's unwillingness to forgive an unforgiving person is motivated by love and a commitment to move toward her and not away from her. He will allow her to wander in her sin until she comes face to face with it. She is too stubborn to forgive, but God will not give in. God's intention is to expose the sin so that she will see it for what it is and be shamed and repulsed by it. Thus His unwillingness to forgive her is sometimes the only way He can woo her back to the place where she can genuinely repent and be reconciled to Him and to the offender.[x]

Belinda had it in for Lacey. Lacey thought she was perfect with her long blonde hair and designer clothes. She put on a good front with shy smiles and kind words, but Belinda knew it was a sham. She could not remember when her animosity against Lacey had started, but it had burgeoned into full-blown hatred. Belinda's friends agreed with her that they had to do something to wipe the smile off Lacey's face.

Belinda's lust for revenge began to drive a wedge into the entire youth group. Insidious spirits began to affect parents, committee members, and some church board members. The pastor became aware of the problem, but he did not know what to do about it. He began to fast and pray.

One Saturday night the youth all headed for the fellowship hall in the church basement. Belinda's friends helped her make it look like an accident when, at the top of the stairs, Belinda tripped and bumped violently into Lacey, knocking her down the stairs. Lacey plummeted downward and landed on her back. The pastor heard the commotion and came quickly. Lacey was bruised and had the breath knocked out of her.

The pastor took the youth pastor, Belinda, and Lacey into his office. With tears, he explained to Belinda that her unforgiving spirit had bred jealousy, hatred, and murder. Shocked at what she had become, Belinda repented and asked Lacey to forgive her. The pastor brought the girls out to the rest of the sober, subdued youth group. Belinda confessed her wrong to them, and a prayer meeting broke out. The next morning, the pastor preached on forgiveness, and the entire congregation was reconciled and healed through a sovereign move of God.

When You Are the Offender

Offenders cannot "unspill the milk," but they can clean up the mess! When you are the offender, it is imperative that you remedy the situation as quickly as possible (Matthew 5:23-24). Until you have reconciled with the person you have wronged, your worship is unacceptable, which strains your relationship with God. If the person you offended fails to approach you according to Luke 17 and Matthew 18, you did not get away with your offense. It simply means a longer time in a poor relationship with God. Neglecting or denying the problem leads to hardening of your heart to the sin, then justifying it, and then enlarging the offense. You become a candidate for church discipline.[xi]

A sin against one's neighbor is also a sin against God (Psalm 51:4). When confronted by the one you have wronged, you are obligated to confess the sin to them and to God and to seek forgiveness.[xii] However, the best course of action is to go the person you offended before she confronts you (cp. Luke 17:3; Matthew 5:23-24).

Celia teaches at a school on her church's campus. She was thrilled when her husband let her go back to college. She sacrificed sleep to care for their two preteen daughters, attend classes, and keep up with household duties and teaching obligations. After graduation, she enrolled in the state's teacher credential program.

Celia's weakness is taking tests. Michelle, the school director, knows this and gives Celia permission to go to her office for a book that will help her study for an upcoming test.

Entering the unoccupied office, Celia locates the book and thumbs through it to verify that is what she needs. Suddenly she realizes she has inadvertently picked up the administrators' test manual and there is a section in the back with test answers. Celia's heart begins to pound. She knows she should immediately put the book back on the shelf, but she reasons that having this advantage would alleviate her testing anxiety. Glancing around to insure that the room is empty, she hastily makes copies and then returns the book.

Celia's conscience torments her. One day she leaves her folders unattended and a fellow teacher idly opens one. She recognizes the test papers because she is studying for the same test. She tells Michelle.

Summoned to Michelle's office, Celia is terrified yet relieved. She repents with tears and asks Michelle to forgive her. They pray together. Michelle calls in the teacher who found the papers, and Celia asks her for forgiveness as well. Celia bears the consequence of waiting until the course is offered again, but the mended relationships and her clear conscience are worth it.

The Cost to Both Parties

Both parties of the forgiveness issue pay a price; neither the offended nor the offender gets off free. The one offended must give up a desire for revenge, cancel the debt, and seek reconciliation. The offender must face what she did with no excuses and make a humble confession. She must accept full responsibility for her actions and change her behavior. She must face the resulting consequences and make whatever restitution is necessary.[xiii] If at any point in the process either party breaches a promise, it can be destructive, and the damage may be twice as hard to repair.

Developing a Spirit of Forgiveness

When we step onto the treadmill of unforgiveness, we trudge through most or all of a ten-step cycle:

1. We feel wronged, whether or not the trespass was intentional. Our hurt is a byproduct of *our reaction* to a

circumstance, event, situation, or conversation.

2. We have difficulty dealing with our hurt; we struggle with lingering feelings.

3. Needing relief, we try to distance ourselves from the pain with substitutes for forgiveness, such as excusing, apologizing, or minimizing.

4. When we cannot outmaneuver our pain, we try to bury it. We refuse to talk about it.

5. We feel defeated—the offender has scored a victory. We seethe with bitterness and resentment. We begin to develop an unforgiving spirit.

6. We become defiled. Our unforgiving spirit taints our relationships and we are less willing to give and receive love.

7. Bereft of peace, we become discouraged about life. We may succumb to clinical depression.

8. As the pain nags at us we are desperate for a way out of our misery. In this vulnerable state we are likely to act irrationally.

9. *The decisive step.* Either we enter into destructive behavior, such as becoming addicted to drugs, alcohol, or sleeping pills, or move away, get divorced, or commit suicide. *Or,* we at last come to our senses and attempt to discover the root cause of our pain. We turn to God, prayer, church, and Bible study for solace and relief from our pain.

10. We begin to deal with the cause of our pain for what it is—a state of unforgiveness. We experience deliverance from our pain as we forgive.[xiv]

Unfortunately, some stay on the treadmill for years. The good news is that with God's help and with practice we can move directly from step one to step ten by developing a forgiving spirit through prayer, a desire to obey God's Word, and through the enabling power of the Holy Spirit.

One key to developing a forgiving spirit is to ask God to help us see His divine purpose in adverse or hurtful events. God allows these things for specific reasons, all of which can eventually work for our good. Joseph endured a series of extremely painful experiences, yet he told his brothers that it was God, not they, who had brought him to Egypt, and that even though the brothers had thought they were doing an evil thing, God meant it for good (Genesis 45:8; 50:20).

When God allows us to suffer offenses, He could be working in the life of the person who wronged us. Or He could be strengthening a weak area in our own life. Or He could be prompting us to develop a forgiving spirit!

Conclusion

No, I'm not perfect. No one is. Relationships can unravel at a bewildering rate until they are hanging by a thread. True forgiveness, modeled after the way God forgives, is how relationships can be knit back together. Make a commitment to begin developing a forgiving spirit today.

[i]Adams, Jay, *From Forgiven to Forgiving, learning to forgive one another God's way,* Calvary Press, Amityville, N.Y., 1994.

[ii]Ibid.

[iii]Ibid.

[iv]Stanley, Charles, *Experiencing Forgiveness, enjoy the peace that comes from giving and receiving it,* Thomas Nelson Publ., Nashville, TN., 1996.

[v]Adams, Jay

[vi]Acts 17:11 Bible Studies, www.acts17-11.com

[vii]Stanley, Charles

[viii]Ibid.

[ix]Ibid.

[x]Herrick, Greg, Ph.D., *The Issue of Forgiveness in the Sermon on the Mount,* Bible Studies Foundation, www.bible.org.

[xi]Adams, Jay

[xii]Ibid.

[xiii]Jackson, Tim

[xiv]Stanley, Charles

CHAPTER FOURTEEN

I've Fallen and I Can't Get Up

OVERCOMING DEPRESSION

As a child, I thought I could whip the world. All I needed was my play gun and holster, a make-believe horse and a vivid imagination. Even as a teenager, I dreamed of having my own ranch, raising horses and cattle, and conquering the western frontier. This was with much influence from Gene Autrey, Roy Rogers, My Friend Flicka, Rin Tin Tin, and Hopalong Cassidy. Of course, many of you will not have a clue of what I am talking about, but I know some of you will.

After having received the Holy Ghost and getting baptized at the age of ten, somewhere in my teen years I began to think that perhaps the mission field would be just the ticket. That seemed to offer adventure and I would also be able to do something for the kingdom of God. Whatever I was going to do, I was not going to do it half-heartedly; I was going to give it one hundred percent.

Being raised in home missions all my life, and having dreams of my own, I knew home missions or being involved in the ministry was not in the plan I had. My mother and father sacrificed for years and that was not going to be the life for me. As I told my mother, "I have given the first part of my life to the ministry; I don't intend to do this with the rest of my life."

Even in all of my self-sufficiency and selfish attitude, somewhere there was a tender spot for the work of God and a compassion for people. I cannot put a date or time on it, but somewhere along the way I began to let God do a work within me. God helped me dredge through all the feelings that had developed over the years and helped me see that there is fulfillment and pleasure to be found when doing His work.

The confidence and drive God placed within my heart found me following the path to the most wonderful man in the world, my husband. Since our marriage, I have been privileged to be a part of a ministry that has been the most challenging and rewarding opportunity I could have been given. I cannot begin to recount all the wonderful miracles I have seen God do and all the blessings He put into my life because of His work. If we truly have a desire to live and work for God, nothing can stop us. The joy of seeing lives changed, hearts mended, and hopes fulfilled cannot be replaced by anything outside of the kingdom of God.

My World Caved In

But then, something happened. I did not see it coming and I do not know how it happened. Somewhere along the road I lost my way, with no sense of direction and no idea how to get back. Feelings of depression invaded my life, not just for a day, but for weeks that turned into months. Fear gripped my heart and mind, afraid that someone would find out and the world around me would turn its back on me.

I felt my world was caving in and I could not keep it from happening. It seemed the only way out was to escape! Being too "chicken" to consider suicide, the thought of running away appealed to my senses.

"If I can just find a place to go," I thought, "start my own life, leave everything here behind, then I will feel better." Looking around my beautiful home I could not understand why I was not content. I had a wonderful husband, the greatest children, a ministry that touched the lives of many. But I felt lost and alone in the world. What was wrong?

Perhaps, I thought, a trip to my dad's would fix the problem. Two days turned into three, three days into a week, a week into three weeks. My husband would call and ask, "When are you coming home?" My answer was, "In a day or so." Finally, I had to make a decision. Would I go back or would I run?

On the way from my dad's house, I stopped to visit with a friend, not intending to say anything about how I was feeling. One thing led to another, and I dumped all the garbage that was in my mind and heart into her living room and her open and willing ears.

Just talking to someone helped it not seem so enormous. I had been trying to keep the depression hidden and it was killing me. I had already gone to the doctor for medication but that only seemed to cover up my feelings, not help me deal with them.

Perhaps you have already noticed a missing ingredient in all of this rambling. Where had I put God? Where was He in my life? How did I come to this place without realizing that I had misplaced Him? After all, I was a pastor's wife; I was in leadership. How did this happen? "Except the LORD build the house, they labour in vain that build it" (Psalm 127:1). I was working in the Lord's house but not letting the Lord build my house!

I do not know where you are in your life right now, but if you are feeling alone, lost, forsaken and confused, please understand that you are not alone in how you feel. Let me tell you that there is hope, there is help, and you can make it through this!

Women in ministry are especially vulnerable to the spirit of depression. There are many factors that play into this. Women have talked to me who felt stretched between family, church, job, and being a wife. All of these areas take a toll on us spiritually, emotionally, and physically. It is of utmost importance to plan on taking some time for refueling or you will find yourself running on empty and get stalled along the way. My husband and I had an agreement. If I said, "I'm going to Memphis for the day and night," he automatically knew I needed some time away. What a blessing those times of being alone were.

There Is Hope and Help

I want to talk about depression and help you see there is hope, there is help, and you are not alone. Depression can be a result of sin; but before you assume you have a spiritual problem, consider the possibility that your depression could be from sickness, hormonal imbalance, or fatigue. (Source: Safe Haven (2003) *Biblical Steps for Overcoming Depression.* Retrieved April 11, 2003: *http://bravewc.com/haven/biblestudies/dep/*.)

Depression can be a consequence of sin in your life, and you need to look at any areas of your spiritual life that need to be addressed. (Source: Safe Haven.) Psalm 147:3 says, "He healeth the broken in heart, and bindeth up their wounds." Don't despair or be afraid. There are ways to receive assistance for all of these, including spiritual and professional help.

As a counselor friend of mine stated, depression comes in many shapes and sizes. Perhaps it is as simple as a mild case of the blues that just will not go away or a severe episode that debilitates you. Not only must you consider the varying degrees of depression, but you must also consider the spiritual and physical aspects as well. (Source: Blash, Daniel, General Statement and Definition Paper.)

Because there are many forms and degrees of depression, it is critical to determine the source of your feelings. Then you learn how to manage your emotions. Listed below are some treatments and where to look for help generally appropriate for dealing with specific causes of depression:

- ❀ *Physical* (hormones, illness, etc.): treated by a doctor
- ❀ *Emotional* (past issues, low self-esteem, etc): treated by a mental health professional
- ❀ *Mental/Cognitive* (thinking problems, poor decision making skills): treated by a health professional
- ❀ *Environmental* (home or work life): treated by a social worker
- ❀ *Spiritual*: treated by the church

According to the *Diagnostic Statistical Manual, Volume IV* (Diagnostic and Statistical Manual of Mental Disorders, DSMIV, American Psychological Association), there are common signs and symptoms for depression:

Low energy

Irritable

No desire to be involved in activities

Mental anguish

Aches and pains

Self-destructive (everyone would be better off if I were not around)

Despairing and hopeless

Difficulty sleeping or sleeping all the time
Withdrawn
Low self-worth
Loss of appetite
Pessimistic about the future
Sad (tearfulness)

As I read through this list, I understand that I had many of these symptoms and wonder how I made it through. The only way was by the prayers of my family and friends. I thought I was hiding my problem, but it was bleeding through every area of my life. Thank God for surrounding me with people who were sensitive and caring.

Learning to Commit

Here are some suggestions to help during times of depression: (Source: Blash.)

* ❀ *Commit to praying first about everything.* Make it a habit to take everything you do to Him in prayer.
* ❀ *Commit to an intimate relationship with God* (James 4:7; Romans 8:16; Philippians 4:7). This has to be worked out between you and God, not what someone else does for their life.
* ❀ *Commit yourself to the renewing of your mind* (Romans 12:2). Only by renewing our minds through His Spirit can we prove what is the good and acceptable and perfect will of God.
* ❀ *Commit yourself to meaningful relationships.* Be sure to surround yourself with people who will be uplifting and positive.
* ❀ *Commit yourself to overcome every loss.* We all suffer loss of different types in our lifetime. It is up to us to deal with them and overcome them. No one else can do it for you.

When a Friend Needs Help

Perhaps you are not battling with depression yourself but you know someone who is. There are ways you can help your friend or loved one suffering from depression. Read through these and give them your support and help. (Source: Blash.)

> ❈ *Build a network of support around the person.* The network should be made up of people who are solid in the faith and who will not be easily drawn into depression themselves.

> ❈ *Maintain firm but fair standards of behavior for the depressed person.* Depression can be debilitating, but in many cases is not. Do not drop your level of expectation just because the person is depressed. The depressed person must be proactive.

> ❈ *Your friend should be trying to help herself as much as you are trying to help her.* Hold her accountable to be faithful to church and other church related activities.

Know your limitations. Use care and caution as you are working with someone who is depressed. At the first hint of self-harm or the harm of others, get professional help. Everyone and every situation is different and interventions will not work in every case. Do not deal with tough cases alone but build a referral network for yourself. The network should include at least one mental health professional.

The most dangerous period of depression is when the person is coming out of depression. Keep a close eye on her until she has achieved full recovery. (Source: Blash.) You can make a difference; let God lead you as you help.

God's Word Gives Strength

You can find great strength and help through the Scriptures. There are many verses in the Bible that can help during times of depression: (Source: Safe Haven.)

- "My soul melteth for heaviness: strengthen thou me according unto thy word" (Psalm 119:28).
- "Purge me with hyssop, and I shall be clean: wash me, and I shall be whiter than snow. Make me to hear joy and gladness; that the bones which thou hast broken may rejoice. Hide thy face from my sins, and blot out all mine iniquities . . . Restore unto me the joy of thy salvation; and uphold me with thy free spirit" (Psalm 51:7-9, 12).
- "Cast thy burden upon the LORD, and he shall sustain thee: he shall never suffer the righteous to be moved" (Psalm 55:22).
- "From the end of the earth will I cry unto thee, when my heart is overwhelmed: lead me to the rock that is higher than I" (Psalm 61:2).
- "Wherefore take unto you the whole armour of God, that ye may be able to withstand in the evil day, and having done all, to stand" (Ephesians 6:13).
- "But they that wait upon the LORD shall renew their strength; they shall mount up with wings as eagles; they shall run, and not be weary; and they shall walk, and not faint" (Isaiah 40:31).

I must tell you there are times I still have to work at staying on top of things. But I am at the place now where I know when it is coming and know what to do and to whom I should turn. If you are going through depression, my prayer is that God surrounds you with people who know your situation and will hold you up in prayer. Do not be afraid to seek help. You do not have to be alone. God has someone special to help you right where you are.

"Be strong and of a good courage, fear not, nor be afraid . . . for the LORD thy God, he it is that doth go with thee; he will not fail thee, nor forsake thee."

DEUTERONOMY 31:6

References

By Faith Only (2003) *Overcoming Depression and Burnout.* Retrieved March 24, 2003. Jackson, Michigan.
http://byfaithonly.com/Overcoming Depression2.html

Safe Haven (2003) *Biblical Steps for Overcoming Depression.* Retrieved April 11, 2003.
http://bravewc.com/haven/biblestudies/dep/

Pathways to Promise (2003) *Working with People with Mental Illness.* Retrieved June 25, 2003. St. Louis, Missouri.
http://www.pathways2promise.org/family/themes.htm

CHAPTER FIFTEEN

From Desolation to Beauty

FINDING HEALING WHEN SEXUALLY ABUSED

*T*he road of life can be fraught with unexpected trials and temptations, ordeals that can send us reeling off our intended course and distort our outlook. In the parable of the Good Samaritan we read of a traveling man who is attacked by thieves on his journey from Jerusalem to Jericho. The Scripture says that this incident leaves the man stripped, wounded, and in a half-dead state (Luke 10:30).

Sexual abuse can affect its victims in much the same way. It is a cruel invasion into the normal flow of life, robbing individuals of their innocence and trust. Hearts can become filled with anger, bitterness, and unforgiveness. In the Old Testament, the story of Tamar and Amnon speaks poignantly about this kind of devastating encounter. The Bible describes Tamar as being "lovely" and "a virgin." Regrettably, her beauty makes her the object of her half-brother's obsessive lust. When she is asked to bring food to Amnon's bedside, the Bible says he "took hold of her and said to her, 'Come, lie with me, my sister.'" Though Tamar pleaded with him, "he would not heed her voice; and being stronger than she, he forced her and lay with her." In just a few terrible moments, her innocence was lost, her life was shattered, and Scripture says that she lived as a "desolate" woman in Absalom's house (II Samuel 13, NKJV).

Desolate in the Father's House

Today, a multitude of often "silent sufferers" are sitting desolate in the Father's house. Outwardly, they may appear to live a charmed life; inwardly they are a wasteland. Many of them would identify themselves as marred vessels—unfit for the Master's use. Somewhere in life the weapon of sexual abuse has been formed against them. Whether it occurred once, as in Tamar's case, or repeatedly over a long period of time, sexual abuse has delivered a crushing blow to their soul. The wounds of sexual abuse can be deep and devastating, but the good news is that "no weapon formed against you shall prosper" (Isaiah 54:17, NKJV). The Hebrew word *tsalach*, translated prosper, means that no weapon formed against you will be successful in accomplishing its goal; it will not advance or be profitable!

This cherished promise has become a living reality in my personal life. At the age of fifteen, rape was my introduction to sexual intimacy. I realize now that for many years I lived in a state of shock or a "half-dead" state. My young naïve mind could not really grasp what had happened to me. The betrayal was harsh, and penetrated to the core of my being, yet I continued along the road of life as though nothing had happened. There were warning signs along the way, but none I was willing to acknowledge or deal with.

It was not until I married that my past crashed headlong into my present life. Something precious had been stolen from me. The gift of sexual purity meant only for my spouse was not there for me to give. Sex is an act of spiritual intensity that is expressly forbidden by God outside the marriage relationship. When His laws are broken, either consensually or through some kind of abuse, future relationships between husbands and wives *will* be affected.

Because memories are called to mind by association, something you hear, see, or smell can bring a memory from your past instantly to mind. With almost the same intensity of the actual assault, memories of the abuse came crashing into the sanctity of my marriage relationship. Initially, those memories threw me into a whirlwind of emotional pain and frustration. Eventually, they drove me to my knees and to a personal search in the Word of God for answers. Ultimately, I experienced God's grace and power in ways I never would have, had I not been afflicted.

Two Immutable Facts

Looking back, I am convinced of two immutable facts: One is that outside of God *any* type of sin is possible; the other is that through Him *any* type of sin can be overcome. Sin is a stain that cannot be removed by anything but the blood of Jesus Christ. This includes the stain of the sins that are committed *against* us.

If sexual abuse has happened to you, it is important to realize that you are not alone, nor is your situation so unique that others could never relate or understand. Believers throughout the ages have felt the sting of this offence. Sexual abuse is one of many trials and temptations referred to in Scripture as "common to man" (I Corinthians 10:13). In his letter to the Hebrews, Paul offers words of encouragement to future hurting believers that someone, somewhere has walked where you have walked and has overcome through faith in the Lord.

"Wherefore seeing we also are compassed about with so great a cloud of witnesses, let us lay aside every weight, and the sin which doth so easily beset us, and let us run with patience the race that is set before us, looking unto Jesus the author and finisher of our faith" (Hebrews 12:1-2).

You may say, but wait a minute! I am the one who has been sinned against; what besetting sins would I have to lay aside? We will talk about that in a moment, but first you must realize that your most blessed assurance comes from knowing that Jesus fully understands, and empathizes with your suffering. "For we have not an high priest which cannot be touched with the feeling of our infirmities; but was in all points tempted like as we are, yet without sin" (Hebrews 4:15). No matter how shattering the abuse and ensuing pain has been, Jesus has in a very real sense walked a mile in *your* shoes.

Scripture reassures that healing awaits you through the liberating truth of His Word. "His divine power hath given unto us all things that pertain unto life and godliness, through the knowledge of him that hath called us to glory and virtue" (II Peter 1:3). Simply put, there is no aspect of your life, no problem you have encountered, to which God's Word does not speak. Victory is certain through your knowledge of Him and by your continued transformation into His image through the power of His Spirit.

The Turning Point

Be encouraged today! Let this moment begin a process of change and deliverance which, until now, you may have considered an utter impossibility. You must purpose in your heart to allow nothing to stand in the way of being made whole. My personal turning point began when I was willing to be honest with myself and with God about what had happened. This includes a willingness to bring your pain out of the darkness and into the light by opening your heart to a trustworthy and godly friend. The Bible says, "Confess your faults one to another, and pray one for another, that ye may be healed" (James 5:16).

It is time for you to take off your mask and be real. Pride and fear can prevent you from exposing your secret struggles. The enemy of your soul plays on these works of the flesh in an attempt to keep you isolated and unable to fulfill God's purpose for your life. He feeds mercilessly on the hurts you have kept hidden in the dark recesses of your heart. He wants to convince you that your situation is hopeless; that people will reject you and look upon you with repulsion. He tells you that you will never get beyond the sting of abuse. But when you honestly and unashamedly bring your pain out of secrecy into the light of truth, you bring one of Satan's most effective devises to a screeching halt. He can no longer use it against you.

As you release your pain to God, and allow a trusted saint or minister to bind together with you in prayer, the anointing begins to destroy the yoke of sexual abuse. Shedding tears at the feet of Jesus brings a release and a healing balm that cannot be found anywhere else. What is accomplished during these special times of anointed prayer cannot be overstated. God's Spirit cleanses the areas of your soul that have been wounded by the weapon of abuse and sets in motion the renewal process that brings change and restoration.

When you surrender your desolate heart to Jesus and turn to His Word with single-hearted faith, the Spirit of truth will begin to reveal any harmful strongholds in your thought life. This is where the weights and besetting sins come in. It is not the abuse itself, but what you have told yourself about the abuse that holds you captive to your past and poisons your present life. The enemy has used the abuse to shoot his fiery darts into your thoughts. He has inundated your mind with imaginations that contradict the truth of God's Word. You, in turn, have listened to his lies and embraced them as your reality. Perhaps you have convinced yourself that if God really loved you, He would never have allowed this to happen. Maybe you have vowed to never let anyone get close enough to hurt you again. You may have convinced yourself that you are a victim and waived your God-given responsibilities in many areas of your life. Perhaps you have unrealistic expectations of your husband, thinking he should be the one to compensate for the horrible thing that has happened to you; consequently, you have become cold and unresponsive in your marriage. It could be you have told yourself you cannot forgive your offender and the absence of forgiveness has turned into a crippling root of bitterness. Whatever your particular situation may be, embracing these lies is what hinders your victory over the abuse.

The End of My "Self"

It was only when I had finally come to the end of my self that God breathed into my troubled soul three life-changing scriptures. At the time, I was still holding fast to my victim status. When that first scripture dropped into my heart it was, indeed, sharper than a two-edged sword! In fact, I did not believe it was the Lord because it seemed rather harsh. But as I sat there broken and undone, He continued to speak and I knew He was giving me something that would be life-changing. These piercing yet liberating truths from God's Word have been fundamental to my personal victory. Healing did not come overnight, but progressively I yielded myself to God and allowed truth to override the lies embedded in the stain of abuse.

The first is found in Romans 6:12: "Therefore do not let sin reign in your mortal body, that you should obey it in its lusts" (NKJV).

The wounded heart naturally craves love and understanding. But although God cares deeply about your pain, He understands the dangers of living in a perpetual "victim mentality." This scripture calls us to be responsible for our own actions, for our *response* to the abuse. Sexual abuse is an offence. The word offence in its original Greek form, *skandalon*, describes the trigger or snare of a trap. Satan uses offences to lure people into emotional traps or strongholds. The natural or carnal mind easily justifies sinful thoughts and responses when an offence has occurred. But the Scripture tells us "the weapons of our warfare are not carnal." God's answer for the wounded soul is to "be transformed by the renewing of your mind" (Romans 12:2, NKJV). This simple truth makes perfect sense when you consider the battle for victory is, in fact, being waged in your mind. When you allow sin to reign through negative responses such as self-pity, withholding love from others, or angry outbursts, you are effectively hindering God's divine intervention.

Through the power of the Holy Ghost you have the God-given ability to respond biblically to whatever God or man does or says. In other words, the Holy Ghost gives us "respond-ability." Romans 6:12 makes us aware of the part we play in overcoming the offence of abuse. It also impacts us with the understanding that rather than merely dealing with the *symptoms* of a problem, God's way targets the *source*. The root of sexual abuse can easily be identified as sin. Similarly, the root of our actions and responses to the abuse are often sinful. As much as Jesus identifies with your anguish, His greatest concern is how you respond to it. If you allow your carnal nature to reign, your life will be ruled by negative emotions. Consequently, your spiritual growth and your ministry cannot develop. Healing and transformation come as you *choose* to put off your carnal responses and allow yourself to be conformed to the image of Jesus Christ. Only He can heal a wounded heart because only Jesus can cleanse and empower you to live victoriously over sin.

The Choice of Forgiveness

The second scripture is found in II Corinthians 5:10: "For we must all appear before the judgment seat of Christ; that every one may receive the things done in his body, according to that he hath done, whether it be good or bad."

No matter how overwhelming your experience has been, you cannot use it as an excuse to think or act in a way that does not glorify God. His Word clearly conveys how we are to respond in the face of evil. Though it goes totally against the grain of our human nature to forbear and forgive one another, God has called us to overcome evil with good (Romans 12:21).

The choice not to forgive has kept many victims of sexual abuse yoked to their past. The Scriptures speak of "imaginations," or thinking that "exalteth itself against the knowledge of God" (II Corinthians 10:5). The knowledge of God says, "But if you do not forgive men their trespasses, neither will your Father forgive your trespasses" (Matthew 6:15, NKJV).

Carnal reasoning that withholds forgiveness must be "cast down" and "every thought brought into captivity to the obedience of Jesus Christ." Your heart may rebel against such words, but I assure you that spending time at the foot of the cross will change how you think about your offender and the offence. When you look at the cross, you see the forgiving face of God; you see human possibilities beyond your own experience. It will expose the veil of flesh that has prevented the glory of God from being revealed in your life and usher into your heart a deep humility. It may seem like a daunting task, but take heart, "the weapons of our warfare are . . . mighty through God to the pulling down of strong holds." Your victory *will* come as you pray, fast, and humbly submit to God's Word.

When you *choose* to forgive, you are casting the heavy weight of sexual abuse upon the Lord and releasing the offender into His capable and just hands. By doing this you are saying, "Jesus, I love you, and I am willing to die to my 'self' to prove it. I give You my pain, and ask You to cleanse and renew the ravaged areas of my heart. Let all of my thoughts, my responses, and my words be an act of worship to You!"

A Place of Contentment

The third scripture is found in Philippians 4:11-12: "For I have learned, in whatsoever state I am, therewith to be content. I know both how to be abased, and I know how to abound: every where and in all things I am instructed both to be full and to be hungry, both to abound and to suffer need."

This final verse really expresses the result of obedience to the first two scriptures. The Greek word for *content* literally expresses a sufficiency in oneself. But here it denotes sufficiency, not in self, but in God. It describes a place of contentment where one becomes independent of external circumstances. This will happen as you begin to turn your eyes fully upon the Lord and believe with all your heart the truth of His loving provision.

The place of contentment is the place of trust. David wrote in Psalm 131, "Surely I have calmed and quieted my soul, like a weaned child with his mother; like a weaned child is my soul within me" (NKJV). The image is that of a child who is no longer unsettled and discontent, but one who is at peace and trusting in his mother. I encourage you to adopt this attitude, to cast aside your own understanding of what has happened in your life, and to trust in the

Lord with *all* of your heart. When you are truly convinced that *all* things do, indeed, work together for good to those who love the Lord, the offence of abuse will lose its sting.

The same word used to describe Tamar's desolation in II Samuel is used in Isaiah to describe the desolation of Zion. God's promise to Zion breathes hope into the heart of the victim of sexual abuse: "O you afflicted one, tossed with tempest, and not comforted, behold I will lay your stones with colorful gems, and lay your foundations with sapphires. I will make your pinnacles of rubies, your gates of crystal, and all your walls of precious stones" (Isaiah 54:11-12, NKJV). In other words, He will turn your desolation into something beautiful. He will restore you! What He has done for the desolate land, He can do for the desolate soul!

As the Holy Ghost uproots the binding strongholds in your life, room is made for the peaceful fruit of righteousness. Bitterness and resentment fade under the awesome power of love; joy lifts the heaviness of depression and self-pity; peace transcends anxiety; impatience gives way to longsuffering; goodness obliterates the desire for revenge; fear and unbelief are cast down by faith; stubbornness and pride are exchanged for meekness; and self-control begins to prevail in the weak areas of your life. The wounds that have nearly destroyed your soul will be turned into a weapon of healing and deliverance in the lives of other hurting souls. May your heart echo with mine the words of David in Psalm 30:11-12 (NKJV):

"You have turned for me my mourning into dancing;
You have put off my sackcloth and
clothed me with gladness,
To the end that my glory may sing praise to You
and not be silent.
O LORD my God, I will give thanks to You forever."

CHAPTER SIXTEEN

All in One Basket

A LOOK AT ADDICTIVE BEHAVIORS

"Many a humble soul will be amazed
to find that the seed it sowed in weakness,
in the dust of daily life, has blossomed into immortal
flowers under the eye of the Lord."
—HARRIET BEECHER STOWE

omen are unique creations of God. Behaviorists and psychologists find subtle differences in the way males and females are wired, not just anatomically, but in terms of thinking, values, and needs. Traditionally, women have been the caregivers in society. You will not read about many wars begun by a woman! First, who wants to sleep in a trench on the ground? We will not go into other inconveniences. No, the pain would not bother us much—not after facing childbirth! But a latrine—are you nuts?

No, women are unique. Women cry more than men, release their feelings, and use language to express in vivid terms—no grunts or noncommittal yes's or no's—so we live longer. You would think they would learn! Hmmm.

But, just like anything on this earth since Adam and Eve decided to go one better on God, there is always a downside, a negative; and for women, that means thinking with the heart unless trained to think with the head. The problem with thinking exclusively with the heart is that "the heart is deceitful above all things, and desperately wicked: who can know it?" (Jeremiah 17:9). I am not trying to give a negative message, because thinking with the heart has made women the linchpin of social orders from the beginning of time. But heart thoughts are deceitful in that they rely a lot on the *sixth sense* women possess, the ability to read others' emotions, facial expressions, and thoughts. In turn, those thoughts turn happenings into the "stuff" of happiness. So, if what is happening to me is negative, then my heart tells me that things are bigger than I can handle.

All In One Basket

This is often where addictive behaviors come into play. We do what we do to get away from feeling what we feel. It is that simple. There are many addictive behaviors, and the bad news is that they are really in one basket. Compulsive behaviors come in many sizes, shapes, and colors. Like any great river, there has to be a starting point; a place that may only be a babbling brook, a line of water coming down the mountainside. But, in time, it gathers momentum, adding other sources of water until it becomes a mighty river. The same is true of compulsive behaviors. Alcoholics do not start out thinking they will be one. Drug addicts always feel they can stop at any time. But the truth is that once addictive behaviors pass a point of no return, you are caught in a net like a fly in a spider web. And the end result is often that *individuals with addictive behaviors usually have low self-esteem and feel anxious if they do not have control over their environment.*

The Bible is a very honest picture of human behavior at its best and at its worst. The characters can easily be seen in our own world with very little change other than place and name. Think of the woman at the well. She was a very needy, insecure woman. Jesus recognized the real source of her problem when He asked her to go and get her husband. Her reply was honest and transparent—I do not have a husband. Jesus took the scenario further and let her know that He knew she had been married to five different men and the one she was with was not her lawful husband! Talk about addiction. But the amazing thing was that Jesus knew she needed to see herself through someone else's eyes and the picture He gave her was the one that showed her what she could be.

How addictive is sin? Proverbs 26:11 says that just like a dog will return to its vomit so a "fool" returns to do more foolishness. One reason for this goes all the way back to the Garden of Eden, and that is the sense of control or choice a person can feel when they do something regardless of the consequences. The reason for this is that these behaviors may produce beta-endorphins in the brain, which makes the person feel "high." Continuing to engage in the activity to achieve this feeling of well-being and euphoria may get a person into an addictive cycle even though it may have negative health or social consequences. The Bible talks about making tough choices in Hebrews 11:25, when it tells us about the difficult decision Moses made: "Choosing rather to suffer affliction with the people of God, than to enjoy the pleasures of sin for a season." God knows what makes this body of ours tick and anything out of balance can have serious consequences mentally, physically, and spiritually.

A Heart Matter

A closer look at addictive behaviors shows that they work off of the five senses humans possess: touch, taste, smell, sight, and hearing. Think about the first story about two people in the Bible. The world was perfect. No rainy days to get them down—just beautiful harmony. Anything they wanted to touch, taste, smell, see, or hear was good. Even the tree in the middle of the garden that God created was beautiful to the eyes and appetizing to eat. It fit all the criteria of the senses. Problem was, God said, No! That is a problem for compulsive humans, is it not? I do not know how many times Eve circled the garden and edged closer and closer to the tree. I do not know how many times she pondered in her *heart*, wondering what was the big deal about this? It doesn't look any different from the trees we usually can eat from, she may have thought. Trouble with the heart is that once you begin thinking with it, you can pretty much talk away common sense. After all, if you are thinking with the senses (for that is the heart and out of it flows all the issues of life), then you can make a case for just about anything.

Addictions, then, come first from the heart. They are often the result of a greater psychological, spiritual, or physical need that has become a source of pain, humiliation, or failure. Therefore, they "act out" these addictions as a type of band-aid or salve to cover the hurt or pain. Some more common addictive behaviors are:

- ❀ Drug and alcohol abuse
- ❀ Sexual abuses against innocent victims, including pornography
- ❀ "Shop 'til you drop" credit card abuse
- ❀ Gotta' have more—I want it all!
- ❀ Food bingeing
- ❀ Controlling—my way or the highway syndrome
- ❀ Extreme need to be right or perfect

❀ Screaming and forms of child or spousal abuse
❀ Anger
❀ Depression, worry, fear

Well, It is Legal, Is It Not?

Usually, we try to think of addictions as only those things that are external, such as smoking, drinking, and drug addictions—these are the bad guys. But you know something? Just because it is legal to do does not make it right to God or healthy for you. Let us look at a real tender issue, obesity. We do not drink. We do not smoke, chew, or roll our own "wacky tobacky"; but we sure can eat! And, take a good hard look at yourself. Do you like what you see? Strangely, Jesus never said anything overtly about smoking, but he covered gluttony pretty thoroughly.

The Internet can make sin a very hidden "private" issue in some ways. We are told that pornography is the largest single use of the Internet, a treasure trove of perversion to people who have tried to keep in check that addictive behavior. Now, in the privacy of their home, in the silence of a room, in the prison of their mind, men and women can feast their souls on perversions and addictions that lead to losses of family, sometimes careers, and certainly respect.

What of the woman or man who cannot stay out of the store, the flea market, or away from the car dealer? The newest car, the latest dress or suit, that antique I just have to have—all those can become addictive behaviors. Now, if you go to the mall after you read this chapter, try not to think of yourself as having an obsessive-compulsive disorder! The good news is that you may really be ok! But, if you have to shop every week or two, spend at least a good part of your income on something new, you could be addicted. I do not want to downplay this with too much humor. Marriages and families have been financially bankrupted by those who just have to have the "newest" gadget, toy, or dress; or, they cause such a commotion and give extreme pain to the other family members until they get what they want. Some are willing to have a trade-off; they will work another job to pay for their binges at the mall. That is an addiction!

The Cover-up

Let us look at the triggers of addictions. They do not just pop up one day. Rather, they often are results of events that happen that create a need for a cover. Think of Adam and Eve again. When they sinned and knew that God knew, what did they do? They covered themselves with fig leaves. I am not sure if I ever met a fig leaf that can do that job convincingly, but hey, it was just God, right? That is how crazy the human mind can be; as if God did not know that they looked pretty silly with fig leaves all over them. I often wondered if they had tape, glue, or Velcro! Nevertheless, they tried the first cover up, and as usual, it did not work.

What was the fruit of that forbidden tree? Not apples, oranges, or lemons—although it could be debated that she was sold a lemon! It was the "fruit of the knowledge of good and evil." Eve knew that knowledge was power and the devil really played that one up to her. She wanted to know what God knew. The old saying, "absolute power corrupts absolutely," could work here. To know what God knows— WOW! What a power trip! What a high! What an addiction! And from that point on, it takes work to do things in moderation; to practice self-restraint and self-discipline.

Getting Out of the Trap

We have talked about what addiction is and where it comes from, but what can one do if one feels trapped in addictive behaviors?

First, identify the addiction and ask yourself why you, an intelligent, God-loving person, allow yourself to be held in the grip of that behavior. Remember to stop thinking of behaviors in a ranking order. They are all in one basket—unhealthy, destructive, tyrannical, and out of balance. Drug abuse falls way down on the list? Do not fall into that trap. They all have the same source—come from the same seeds—originate in the same place—the heart.

Second, admit that you are addicted and begin to find help for your problem. That may be your pastor, your spouse, or family. But, do seek help. There are Christian counselors who can give you professional guidance as well, and sometimes we need to go a little deeper to find out why we choose to self-destruct.

Third, remember that all behavior can be modified through the blood of Jesus Christ and through not repeating the behavior. Nature abhors a vacuum, so when you stop behaving in a destructive way, remember to fill that need with something good, something healthy, something positive, or you may return to self-destructive behavior. Go to school. Volunteer at the hospital or nursing home. Join Literacy Volunteers and teach people to read. You can only be doing one thing at a time, so if you fill that time with positive acts, you will be able to superimpose new habits over the old.

Finally, remember that you are not alone. You are not the only person fighting the battle against addictive behavior. Take courage and realize that you can take control over the five senses you possess. They are yours. It is up to you now.

CHAPTER SEVENTEEN

It Began in Eden

BIBLICAL GUIDANCE FOR EATING DISORDERS

Pop Quiz! (Do not worry—you do know the answers!)

1. Are you happy with the way you look?
2. What do you think when you look in the mirror?
3. How did you form that opinion about yourself?

Very few of us would answer the first two questions in a positive manner. The third question usually takes a little more thought. Nevertheless, most women find themselves wishing their bodies were different. If you are a size 6, there is an infinite drive to stay a size 6 or less. If you are a size 16, there is an overwhelming desire to be a size 14 or 12. If you are tall, you want to be short. If you are short, you want to be tall. If you are medium height, chances are you want to be either tall or short instead of "average." It is a fact of human nature that we are not happy with ourselves as we are.

Unfortunately for us, the advertisers in this world are well aware of our self-dissatisfaction. They parade models before us who, bless their hearts, cannot weigh more than one hundred pounds soaking wet. Ads and billboards across the Western world scream the message, "If you do not look like us, you are just not enough." It is no wonder that women experience a great deal of pressure to look better than they already do.

Let me say at the outset that God did not intend for us to be consistently unhappy or unsatisfied with ourselves. Jeremiah quoted God in Jeremiah 29:11, saying, "For I know the thoughts that I think toward you . . . thoughts of peace, and not of evil, to give you an expected end." What is the "expected end" He is talking about here? Verse 14 says, "I will be found of you, saith the LORD: and I will turn away your captivity." God wants us to be free—free from the captivity or bondage of this world, free from the pressures that try to control us, free from the ideals of this world. The thoughts of mankind are finite when compared to the thoughts of our infinite God: "For my thoughts are not your thoughts, neither are your ways my ways, saith the LORD" (Isaiah 55:8).

As we explore the ins and outs of dieting and eating disorders, please be aware that as the writer of this study I am not the "Dr. Spock" of dietary maintenance, nor am I the food police. I will not tell you when to eat, how to eat, or what to eat. If you are looking for the same approach that you would see at a recovery center for eating disorders, I am afraid you will not find it here. You will find a few simple explanations for why women struggle with eating issues. We will also explore a path toward recovery, one that leads straight into the will of God. Keep in mind that Jesus has our best interests at heart. We look to His Word for guidance and to Him for understanding. I invite you to take a moment right now to pray that God would open your understanding to this, enable you in His power, and that He would draw you into the knowledge of His peace.

⌒

I think I have spent my life on a diet, and I know that I am not alone. It would seem that most women in Western culture can relate to problems with eating. We eat too much; we eat too little; we do not eat often enough; we do not eat the right things. There are many powers involved in the struggle to control food: the media, our individual life situations, the food itself, and the value associated with food. The rising prevalence of eating-related issues has several causes, but undoubtedly the most dominant and most visible is the media. We have touched on this a bit already, but let us take a closer look.

The Powers That So Easily Affect Us

"For we wrestle not against flesh and blood, but against principalities, against powers, against the rulers of the darkness of this world, against spiritual wickedness in high places" (Ephesians 6:12).

The Power of Cultural Influences

When you see advertisements showcasing painfully thin models, take a look at what they are selling. Ads for potato chips, fast food, soda, and other non-nutritional foods are plastered on the sides of buildings and in the windows of bus stops. What a paradox! "Be thin so that you can wear our newest, coolest clothes, but be sure you stop by the convenience store for our 42-ounce soda and a bag of chips for just a few bucks!" It is truly ridiculous!

In fact, for centuries the island nation of Fiji had a population practically immune to eating disorders. The "ideal" body shape for women in Fiji would have been considered "plump" by North American standards. In 1995, however, mainstream television waged a wholesale invasion into the homes of the inhabitants of Fiji. Here are the results of a study done between 1995 and 1998:

"In 1995, the number of girls who self-induced vomiting to control their weight was zero. But three years after the introduction of television, that figure had reached 11%. They also found that dieting had become commonplace. In 1998, 69% of those studied said they had gone on diets to lose weight and 74% said they thought they were 'too big or fat'" (as reported by BBC News Online, *http://news.bbc.co.uk/1/hi/health/2018900.stm*).

This is not to say that the media is entirely responsible for the prevalence of eating disorders, but this type of information does highlight the impact of outside influences on the way women view food. We can assume by the heightened prevalence of purging (self-induced vomiting or use of laxatives) in Fiji that women were willing to take drastic measures to meet the "standard" that was set before them. Here is the question to ask yourself: Were these women happier before they thought they were fat, or after they became thin? What do you think?

The Power of Individual Life Influences

As powerful as the media is in influencing the general consensus, there are other individual influences that can have just as much bearing on whether or not a woman is willing to compulsively diet, starve herself, induce vomiting, or swallow a pack of diuretics in order to lose weight. A teenage boy who comments on how fat his girlfriend is; a mom who worries so much about her child being fat that she neglects to keep her healthy; a father who overemphasizes the thinness of his wife or of actresses and models: all of these situations can push girls over the edge, so to speak. Girls who are involved in sports, especially those who have weight requirements such as gymnastics and ballet, are more likely to engage in bulimic or anorectic behavior. "According to a 1992 American College of Sports Medicine study, eating disorders affected 62 percent of females in sports such as figure skating and gymnastics" (as reported by Mirror-Mirror.org, a website dedicated to news about eating disorders).

Let us not forget the flipside of the coin. Even more prevalent than bulimia or anorexia, the phenomena of overeating and obesity are becoming more and more hazardous to women's health. Obesity and bulimia can even coexist, leading to major health complications. The simple fact is that we take many approaches to food that prove to be unhealthy in the long run, both to our physical bodies and to our psychological selves. There are many excellent examples that illustrate this point, but let us consider, for a moment, the first bad encounter a woman had with food.

The Power of Food: One Woman's Story

Eve was created by God Himself. She was placed in a perfect garden, had a perfect husband, and enjoyed a perfect communion with God. As in Adam, God had placed in Eve the desire to be with Him, to be like Him. She wanted to know God, to see God, to hear His voice, to feel His touch, to serve Him in the garden. Her goals revolved around God. She literally had it all together in one neat little package.

And then it happened. It was just an ordinary day as Eve strolled through the garden. She stopped to smell the roses and pet the chipmunks along the way. There were horses galloping alongside the grove of apple trees, and a pair of lions spent their afternoon lazing about in the field. Eve walked toward the river, then sat laughing as the frogs leaped playfully along the banks. When she stood up to go to find Adam, she took one last look at the most curious sight in the neighborhood: a beautiful tree planted right in the middle of her backyard. It still amazed her that God would make this tree off limits. It was very beautiful! Such a tree probably produced the best tasting fruit ever created!

With a sigh, she started to walk away. Then she heard a voice calling to her. "Psssst. Eve! Over here!"

It was not her husband; Adam's voice was much deeper. It was not God; Eve knew His voice, too. She turned to look into the eyes of a snake hanging from a limb of that most beautiful tree. As soon as the snake had her attention, he began to question her: "Did not God say that you cannot eat of every tree of the garden?"

Eve thought back to what Adam had told her about God's rule. "We can eat any fruit in the garden that we want except the fruit from this tree. We cannot even touch it, or else we will die." Eve was pretty sure that is what Adam told her.

The serpent smiled. "Eve, Eve, Eve. Come on now. You are not going to die! Actually it is just that God knows that if you eat of this tree, you are going to be changed! You and Adam will be as gods, and you will know good and evil."

Eve looked at the tree again. It sure was beautiful! And the fruit was ripe and juicy! She could almost taste it. She slowly reached out her hand and touched a piece of fruit. Nothing happened. She looked back at the snake, then plucked the fruit from the tree. She thought, *This is going to make me like God! That is what I have always wanted, and Adam will be very proud of me if I am like God!* She bit into the fruit, then waited. Nothing happened. She took the fruit to her husband, and they both ate. Then, as she turned to look at her husband, something strange happened. She felt a flush fill her cheeks; then she ran and hid behind the nearest bush. She was very ashamed. She was embarrassed by her nakedness. What had she done?

Eve, the first woman ever made, a being fashioned directly by the hand of God (Genesis 2:22), had difficulty with the desirability of food. The very first sin against the Word of God involved food. If there were any doubts about the effect that food can have on a woman, let them be dispelled by this statement: Since the Garden of Eden, women have been in a fight with food!

In addition to struggling with the issue of food itself, Eve (with the help of the serpent) assigned a certain value to the forbidden fruit. She wanted to be like God—a good intention—but she ignored the Word of God in trying to accomplish that goal. She tried to use the wrong method to obtain her goal. However, we do not have to fall prey to Eve's dilemma. God has given us three great keys with which to unlock the prison of our circumstances: an understanding of the emotions behind eating problems, the guidance of His Word, and the opportunity to choose our own path.

Gaining Ground and Fighting Back
Key #1: Understanding Your Emotions

The first key to unlocking the prison of eating disorders and other problems with food is merely understanding what fuels your binges or your starvation. Is there a particular situation that sends you into a frenzy, or a certain person whom you feel pressures you to be different than you are? If you said yes to either of these questions, think about what aspects of that relationship/situation make you crazy. What can you do to control either the situation or your reaction to that person? Can you imagine yourself outside this negative influence? If you can imagine life without this specific stressor, you are one step closer to control of your problem.

Think about the last time you felt depressed or disappointed. Did you eat some chocolate or ice cream to make yourself feel better? Maybe you were depressed because you saw a "fat" person staring back at you in the mirror, so you decided not to eat that day. Either way, you "self-medicated" with food or the lack thereof. You treated your emotional symptoms by controlling your food intake, whether you ate a lot or not at all.

The two most common emotions experienced by women with eating disorders are shame and fear. We are ashamed of the way we look, so we comfort ourselves with food. We are ashamed that we throw up when no one is looking. We fear that someone will figure it out, and we will be held up to the microscope of public scrutiny. We are afraid that we will be too fat, and people will stop loving us.

If these and other emotions drive you to hurt yourself with food, be aware of them. Know when you are starting that downward spiral. Consciously think about your emotional state during a binge or purge.

Key #2: The Gift of Choice

Every individual on this earth has been given the power of choice by God Himself. David said, "I have chosen the way of truth" (Psalm 119:30). Joshua encouraged the people of Israel, "Choose you this day whom ye will serve . . . but as for me and my house, we will serve the LORD" (Joshua 24:15).

God has empowered us to choose, but many times we do not accept that power. We feel locked in an unbreakable cycle of hurt, shame, fear, depression. We do not feel worthy of choice. We do not think God cares about the everyday situations, such as problems with eating. The psalmist said it like this: "What is man, that thou art mindful of him?" (Psalm 8:4). Even though we do not feel worthy, Jesus still considers us to be the "apple of [his] eye" (Psalm 17:8).

In fact, we are made to house the Spirit of God. "What? know ye not that your body is the temple of the Holy Ghost which is in you, which ye have of God, and ye are not your own? For ye are bought with a price: therefore glorify God in your body, and in your spirit, which are God's" (I Corinthians 6:19-20). God has created you to be a worthy temple of His Spirit. And if God has said that we are worthy, who are we to argue?

In our world today, we are all responsible to make our own choices in life, including how we eat. Like Eve, we all make decisions about our food. Eve depended upon human logic to make her decision.

1. She *used her five senses* to determine the level of danger and desirability of the fruit.
2. She *thought* about her options—to eat or not to eat.
3. She *adjusted her attitude* based on the information provided by her senses and her logic.
4. Eve *acted* based on her attitude.

These are the four basic steps involved in the human decision-making process. God has given you the ability to use this process to your benefit. You are not limited to using food to address your problems. There are hundreds of stress-busters that can take the place of the binge-purge cycle. It is not easy, but it is a place to start. Once a stress-buster becomes your habit, the desire to take your stress out on food will grow weaker and weaker day by day.

Think for a moment about how you treat food in relation to your stressors. If a person in your life tends to pressure you to change in a negative way, do you immediately retreat into a bag of chips? Or does a certain situation send you into binge-purge cycle? If you are using food to take away that stress, try to be conscious of other possible stress-reducing behaviors, such as journaling, leaving the room, and engaging in breathing exercises. You may prefer to be more spiritual in your approach. Try prayer and worship. God responds to every prayer, and regardless of our situation, He is always worthy of our worship. If you also need a physical outlet, try crumpling paper, throwing foam balls, or screaming into a pillow.

These are just a few ideas, but there is no limit to what you can do to get rid of emotional stress. As long as your stress-buster does not hurt yourself or anyone else, use it to your benefit. *Sense* what might work for you in a given situation, *think* about your choices, *adjust your attitude* about the options, then *act* accordingly. This process may take five seconds or five minutes to think through, and it might take five weeks, five months, or five years to become completely effective. During that time, it is easy to become discouraged, but God is just waiting to give you the strength to fight back.

Finally, we have come to the most important and powerful key to recovery.

Key #3: The Word of Truth

In every woman's struggle with eating disorders, there are three major emotions in play: shame, fear, and self-loathing. On these issues, God's Word speaks for itself. He sees everything that has happened in your life. He knows every pain, every circumstance.

Regarding shame, God has declared that His children are *not* to be ashamed (Joel 2:26-27). In fact, He provided us an antidote to shame—hope:

> ❈ "And hope maketh not ashamed; because the love of God is shed abroad in our hearts by the Holy Ghost which is given unto us" (Romans 5:5).

❅ "Why art thou cast down, O my soul? and why art thou disquieted within me? hope thou in God: for I shall yet praise him for the help of his countenance" (Psalm 42:5).

God also wants His people to be free from fear, and He has provided an answer for that as well:

❅ "There is no fear in love; but perfect love casteth out fear: because fear hath torment" (I John 4:18).

❅ "The LORD is my light and my salvation; whom shall I fear? the LORD is the strength of my life; of whom shall I be afraid? When the wicked, even mine enemies and my foes, came upon me to eat up my flesh, they stumbled and fell" (Psalm 27:1-2).

God wants us to know that He is on our side. He wants desperately to assist us. Yet it has often been said that God is a gentleman; He will not force you to do anything. And yet He watches you as you suffer through the agony of the binge-purge cycle, of starvation or overeating. The expression on His face says it all: "Just let me help you. Just let me calm your storm. I love you and I want to see you be healthy. Let me help you make the right choices."

One further word of encouragement: "Wait on the LORD: be of good courage, and he shall strengthen thine heart: wait, I say, on the LORD" (Psalm 27:14).

You do not have to deal with eating disorders alone. Depend on God. Talk to your pastor. Seek godly counsel. Be ready for healing and restoration to come as you wait on the Lord.

CHAPTER EIGHTEEN

I've Failed

FORGIVING MYSELF
WHEN GOD ALREADY HAS

To really look at the issue of forgiveness, we need to take a trip all the way back to the beginning when God created human life. Forgiveness has a long history! And the inability of humans to forgive themselves for small or big misdeeds goes back a very long way as well. The very first scriptures tell us about a world with no form, no real image, and no purpose. God's first action established form, image, and purpose. His words, exact and descriptive, pronounced His creation "good." The Grand Canyon—good. Majestic Mount Everest—good. Flowers bursting with colorful energy—good. No angelic oohs and aahs were needed for God to know who He was or to help Him accomplish His plan.

When God created Adam and Eve, He role-modeled a positive identity and built into them awesome capabilities. God deliberately planted His creative and intellectual genius into human nature, and He trusted them to follow

His guidelines. Only Adam and Eve's disobedience tainted and destroyed in human beings the opportunity to repeat God's "good" creative acts. Forcibly expelled from the garden, Adam and Eve began a journey that every human would have to travel. This road now would be one with thorns, thistles, work, toil, suffering, and eventually death. Not one child of Adam has escaped this road. Some have not suffered as much as others, but all travel this route.

Sin destroyed the picture of innocence for every human being, and disobedience inflicted separation from God. There was no Bible, no voice in the garden, just an awful silence that deafened and stifled the original genius of God's special creation. Without God to teach them by example, Adam and Eve created and mastered the art of hiding and blaming. Cheap substitutes such as shame, guilt, subtlety, deceit, violence, and greed covered their naked souls. Without God's image from which to learn, humankind went into a spiritual meltdown from the inside out. Humankind, full of confidence and bursting with knowledge, strolled shoulder to shoulder with God. Now, after they disobeyed, they hunkered down, subjected to a base nature of survival. The strong survived. The weak died.

But, this was not God's original plan. He willed Adam the world! God's opinion was that Adam could absolutely rule the whole earth. Only sin diverted the sacred plan. Noah's flood wiped away the evidence of this first society except for eight souls. Looking at the earth after the flood, it was easy to see that the earth had changed. Unfortunately, humans had not. The flood could not erase the erosion of the human spirit that sin brought to the self-image of man. Just a few generations from Noah, his descendents, still hiding, deceiving, and conniving, devised a plan to outsmart God by contriving to build a tower reaching into the heavens (in which to hide from God's wrath). God, still loving, still believing in the abilities of His creation to accomplish this, confused their tongues because "nothing will be restrained from them, which they have imagined to do" (Genesis 11:6).

One of the major lessons we learn from the people who lived from Adam to Noah is that humans are willful and tend to take the path that leads away from God. That path has dire consequences, some of which happen in circumstances and events, while some are internalized and eat away at the soul.

A Look at Guilt

Let's look honestly at guilt and see how to deal with it. The best and quickest way is to acknowledge that we did something wrong. The Bible is a book of ideals. It sets the standard for what God wants us to do. Even so, God more than all of humanity, understood that people do not always live up to His ideals, His law. That's the whole purpose of His Word, and even more so, the whole purpose of Him coming to earth. Jesus Christ was tempted in every way we are and yet He did not sin. But He had the Spirit of God in Him without *measure*. We have the earnest of our inheritance—just the down payment. He could be perfect, but His journey on this earth made Him vitally familiar with the failings of humanity. He watched Peter rise to spiritual revelation (*Thou art the Christ*) and fall to a tool of the enemy (*Get thee behind me, Satan*) in just a few short verses (Matthew 16:16, 23). He suffered the betrayal of a dear and trusted friend, Judas. His own brothers did not believe in Him even though they heard the stories of His divine birth. Jesus knew all that firsthand and still went to the cross. He was still willing to pay the ultimate penalty.

I've Made a Mistake!

Why do we feel that we have to be perfect all the time, and that we cannot make a mistake? That's not possible. That's right, you say, but I'm a Christian and I should know better. I should listen to God's Word and His Spirit. I'm just disobedient. I'm just stubborn. I'm just . . . whatever! And, it's all those little things we say to ourselves that keep the mournful tunes blasting in our heads. I know that we all want to believe that the Holy Ghost takes every possibility of sin out of us, but that is not the purpose of the Holy Ghost. The purpose is to lead and guide us into all truth! That means we are all on a journey. Roads are funny, aren't they? Sometimes a little shortcut looks inviting, or a new way we've never traveled looks too good to be true, and we take a detour. How many times in life have we had to circle back and get on the main road to make sure we got to our destination? Did you sit there and beat yourself over the head because you took a wrong turn? If you did, you did not get to the place you wanted to go! No, you simply turned around and got your car going the right way. That is the exact way to deal with sin. Turn around and go the right way.

What about those sins that grieve your spirit now that you know God's Word and have begun your journey of faith? Amazing, isn't it, how things we did in our past can come back to haunt us. For women, this is very distressing because we tend to brood more than men do. We experience fear from many angles, but fear based in our memories is the most destructive. I'm thinking of fear that someone we care for will find out something about our past life and will not love us anymore. Women who have lived promiscuous lives with multiple partners, women who have had abortions, and women who have lived with addictive behaviors can live in a state of horror and shame that totally disable their ability to live in the grace of God.

This is not to say you should go around and spread the "good news" of your past life, but neither should you allow the devil to hold you hostage to fear, guilt, and shame. Enough is enough! So that was your life. Now you are walking a new way. Can you change anything that happened in the past? No. Face it; you cannot change it. But, Jesus changed *you*. Get on with your life. What if someone finds out something you don't want anyone to know? Well, first let me say that if anyone is a good friend, they would come and talk to you about what they had heard. If they are not a good friend, they may spread some juicy tidbits around. So people know. Big deal. If we all knew, really knew, each other, we might not be prone to be so friendly with each other. Consider: except for the grace of God, not a *one* of us will make it. And, if someone wants to gossip, they will have to stand and tell God why they said what they did. You are forgiven!

God Intends a Positive Self-Image

God intends for us to have a positive image of ourselves. Some have a problem with using the term self-esteem. But that problem lies in semantics—the difference in the meaning between pride and self-esteem. So, let's define both behaviors.

Pride begins as a lie, an exaggeration. One can be very good at something but still not be able to be the all-time, forever best. Someone, someplace, will break any record set. Athletes may set records that make them champions for a while, but it is just a matter of time until the record will be broken. If self-image is rooted in a record rather than the total person, all that prior success develops into a lasting defeat.

A healthy self-image develops from reality and promotes an honest evaluation and appreciation for specific talents as well as an honest understanding of what is not possible. This holds true whether the evaluation is of one-self or of another. God commanded through Moses that Israel learn to "love thy neighbor as thyself." Jesus reiterated this principle in the New Testament. The implication is very explicit: you cannot love another person unless and until you love yourself.

The crux of the matter lies in this: do you believe that Jesus forgave you? If you do, then walk in that forgiveness. God's grace is sufficient for you and me. The only time it isn't is when you or I refuse to accept it.

Living in God's Grace

What can you do to live in God's grace? Let's look at establishing habits. Behaviorists say that we need to repeat an act at least twenty-one times before the new behavior becomes the norm. So, replace negative thoughts with positive thoughts. Put positive scriptures around your workplace, your home, your car, and let your mind feed on those.

Second, practice good works. You'd be surprised how people will come to the defense of someone who shows kindness to others. Find a community project to volunteer for—not for the church but for YOU! It works. When you begin living the new creation you will begin believing it.

Third, surround yourself with people who affirm you. Stay away from people you cannot trust, regardless of where they are—family, church, work, or school. Just because someone is in one of those social settings does not mean they should be given carte blanche to all your life history or even to your dreams. Learn to establish eye contact with people when you speak to them. Do not lower your eyes or let them dart about the room when you are trying to establish an understanding of your position on an issue. And, feel free to set boundaries. Just breathing does not entitle a person to dominate your life and make you miserable. Learn to take control in situations by establishing some parameters for behavior. If a situation gets out of control, do not be afraid to excuse yourself from that inferno. What are you trying to prove anyway?

My favorite historical female character is Eleanor Roosevelt. Let me tell you why. When Eleanor was born, her parents had wished for a "precious boy" and the little girl was viewed as "a more wrinkled and less attractive baby than the average" by her beautiful socialite mother. She was a very fearful child, "afraid of being scolded" and unliked. She felt inferior to her mother whom she described as "the most beautiful woman she ever knew" but who thought Eleanor was "plain to the point of ugliness." She criticized her constantly and called her "Granny" and apologized to friends that Eleanor "was too 'old-fashioned'." As a small child she wore a back brace for two years to correct a curvature of her spine

When her brothers were born, she later wrote that her mother doted on them and spent little time with her. "I wanted to sink through the floor in shame, and I felt I was apart from the boys."

Her father dubbed her "a miracle from heaven," but he was an alcoholic who could not keep his word to his family or stay away from drink, and he caused immense grief to everyone. The family at one time committed him to an insane asylum and placed his money through the courts into a trust for his family; Eleanor was six at this time. Eventually, he was released but the estrangement created an irreparable rift in the family. Eleanor adored him regardless, but learned early on not to depend on him. However, he adored Eleanor, whom he called "Little Nell," his childhood nickname. Uniquely, he spent much time trying to build her up, to counter the damage inflicted by her mother's disappointment at her plain looks, and gave her strong ideals and presented her with the picture of what *he* wanted her to be—noble, brave, studious, religious, loving, and good.

This woman experienced tragedy on top of tragedy. A young son, one of five children she bore to FDR, died as a young toddler. She found FDR in the midst of a disgusting marital affair with her own personal secretary. And when FDR contracted polio, she nursed him back from the debilitating effects of that disease and propelled him into the political spotlight by campaigning for him, speaking for him, and doing a lot of the work he could no longer do. In spite of these personal disasters, Eleanor persevered and became a force for social change, actually inspiring many of the "New Deal" programs that helped American's make it through the Great Depression. Her favorite and most often quoted statement is this: *"No one can make you feel inferior without your consent."*

Let's recap what we can do to live in God's grace and forgiveness.

❀ Think positively by actively using the Word of God to remind you of God's forgiveness.

❀ Practice good works. Get out of your "own world" to help others who may have many more problems than you have. Volunteer at a hospital, library, women's shelter, a school, food bank, or disaster program.

❀ Do not hang around people who insist on putting you down, regardless of where they may be. "No one can make you feel inferior without your consent."

Self-Esteem Evaluation

Score 0 if not true; 1 if somewhat true; 2 if largely true; 3 if true.

_____ 1. I usually feel inferior to others.

_____ 2. I normally feel warm and happy about myself.

_____ 3. I often feel inadequate to handle new situations.

_____ 4. I usually feel warm and friendly toward all I contact.

_____ 5. I habitually condemn myself for my mistakes and shortcomings.

_____ 6. I am free of shame, blame, guilt, and remorse.

_____ 7. I have a driving need to prove my worth and excellence.

_____ 8. I have great enjoyment and zest for living.

_____ 9. I am much concerned about what people think and say of me.

_____ 10. I can let others be "wrong" without attempting to correct them.

_____ 11. I have an intense need for recognition and approval.

_____ 12. I am usually free of emotional turmoil, conflict and frustration.

_____ 13. Losing generally causes me to feel resentful and "less than."

_____ 14. I usually anticipate new endeavors with quiet confidence.

_____ 15. I am prone to condemn others and often wish them punished.

_____ 16. I normally do my own thinking and make my own decisions.

_____ 17. I often defer to others on account of their ability, wealth, or prestige.

_____ **18.** I willingly take responsibility for the consequences of my actions.

_____ **19.** I am inclined to exaggerate and lie to maintain a desired image.

_____ **20.** I am free to give precedence to my own needs and desires.

_____ **21.** I tend to belittle my own talents, possessions, and achievements.

_____ **22.** I normally speak up for my own opinions and convictions.

_____ **23.** I habitually deny, alibi, justify, or rationalize my mistakes and defeats.

_____ **24.** I am usually poised and comfortable among strangers.

_____ **25.** I am very often critical and belittling of others.

_____ **26.** I am free to express love, anger, hostility, resentment, joy, etc.

_____ **27.** I feel very vulnerable to others' opinions, comments, and attitudes.

_____ **28.** I rarely experience jealously, envy, or suspicion.

_____ **29.** I am a professional people pleaser.

_____ **30.** I am not prejudiced toward racial ethnic or religious groups.

_____ **31.** I am fearful of exposing my "real self."

_____ **32.** I am normally friendly, considerate, and generous with others.

_____ **33.** I often blame others for my handicaps, problems, and mistakes.

_____ **34.** I rarely feel uncomfortable, lonely, and isolated when alone.

_____ **35.** I am a compulsive "perfectionist."

_____ **36.** I accept compliments and gifts without embarrassment or obligation.

_____ 37. I am often compulsive about eating, smoking, talking, or drinking.

_____ 38. I am appreciative of others' achievements and ideas.

_____ 39. I often shun new endeavors because of fears of mistakes or failure.

_____ 40. I make and keep friends without exerting myself.

_____ 41. I am often embarrassed by the actions of my family or friends.

_____ 42. I readily admit my mistakes, shortcomings, or defeats.

_____ 43. I experience a strong need to defend my acts, opinions, and beliefs.

_____ 44. I take disagreement and refusal without feeling "put down" or rejected.

_____ 45. I have an intense need for confirmation and agreement.

_____ 46. I am eagerly open to new ideas and proposals.

_____ 47. I customarily judge my self-worth by personal comparison with others.

_____ 48. I am free to think any thoughts that come into my mind.

_____ 49. I frequently boast about myself, my possessions and achievements.

_____ 50. I accept my own authority and do as I, myself, see fit.

_____ = **Self-Esteem Index (SEI)**

To obtain your Self-Esteem Index, add the individual scores of all even numbered statements. From this total subtract the sum of the individual scores of all odd numbered statements. The net score is your current Self-Esteem Index or SEI. The range is from -75 to +75. Experience shows that any net score under +65 is handicapping; a score of 35 or less is seriously handicapping; and a zero or minus score indicates a truly crippling lack of self-esteem.

CHAPTER NINETEEN

I Will Praise

COPING WITH CHRONIC ILLNESS

Granulomatis colitis. "Okay," I thought. "No big deal. Some people have bad sinuses—I have granulomatis colitis." I had the joyful optimism of youth, the pleasure of a young family, and the knowledge that God was going to lead us to Germany as missionaries. Thankfully, I did not know the road that lay ahead.

The year was 1976. My husband and I had served as short-term missionaries in Jamaica and had loved it. We had two children, were working in the Foreign Missions Division, and were making plans to go to the land to which God had called us before we ever married. Life was truly good.

A few months after our son was born, I started having intestinal bleeding. There were few signs of anything seriously wrong except for this occasional bleeding. My doctor took a biopsy, pronounced that I had granulomatis colitis, but said that there should be no problem being treated in an industrialized country such as Germany. So, we received our missionary appointment and were off!

For the most part, I enjoyed deputation. Pastors and saints alike treated us wonderfully and, a year later, my husband, my six-year-old daughter, two-year-old son, and I were on the plane to Weisbaden, West Germany.

As instructed by my stateside doctor, I immediately found an English-speaking German doctor. The first thing that he did was to take me off all medicine. When I began to have severe cramps, he prescribed large doses of steroids.

Up until now, the disease had been inconvenient but not a real problem. However, with the use of steroids, I became extremely violent. The pivotal day came when my two-year-old said something and I reacted by throwing him against the opposite wall. That did it! The next thing that I threw was the pills into the trash!

At about this time my mother called from Portland, Oregon, to say that she had cancer and was not expected to live long. It is one thing to be sick and quite another to not have your mother to tell you what to do when you are sick. I felt like the rug of life had literally been pulled out from under me.

A Lesson to Learn

What do you do when you are emotionally lying flat on your back with nowhere to go and no place to turn? I learned the most important lesson of my entire life: I learn to praise.

I had grown up in the church. I had married and had my children while faithfully being involved in church. But I had never learned to really praise. It was a lesson that had to be learned now.

I began by praising God for five minutes at a time. I really did not have the faith or strength to do any more than that time frame. Gradually, I could praise for ten and then fifteen minutes. When I got to the place where I could praise for an hour at a time, I thought I was ready to whip all of the demons in hell!

Physically, I was no better. I weighed 97 pounds. I had to stay in bed many days. On days that I could get out of bed, I usually had to hold onto the wall for support—but I had found an artesian well of strength. I had learned how to praise.

One evening, I received the call I had been dreading. Mom was given only a few days to live; if I wanted to see her again on this side of eternity, I should return to the States—pronto!

My mother passed away, leaving my father alone to pastor a church and finish raising a sixteen-year-old daughter. It was a bleak situation. I was ill and I knew it. I had just been in a very stressful situation and was also very lonely for my home. I felt that my physical condition was to be expected. To be perfectly honest, I just wanted to go back to the mission field and my family.

My dad saw the pain I was in and suggested that we just stop by the hospital to get some kind of pain pill to help in making the trip back. That sounded like a good idea. However, the emergency room doctors told me that I had an intestinal blockage that would have to be surgically removed. They called my illness Crohn's Disease. I had never heard of it and began questioning anyone and everyone I could find.

Crohn's is an autoimmune disease that hardens the walls of the colon. It is called the young people's disease, for it normally strikes from the age of sixteen to twenty-four years. There is no cure. In fact, one doctor told me that he would rather tell a patient they had cancer than Crohn's because "at least they will be able to die from cancer; they will just suffer with Crohn's."

This went wrong; that went wrong. I needed to stay just a little longer in the hospital; well, maybe just a little longer. This level needed to be higher before I could go home. That report needed to show some improvement. That first hospital stay was a very long time. But time marched on, and eventually I was able to get on the plane and go to my children whom I had not seen in three months.

When I first went back to Germany, I did some better; but after our move to Southern Germany, it became more of a struggle to feel well. That did not stop me from trying my best to be healthy. I went to language school, continued to supervise my growing family, and tried to help my husband establish a work both among the American military and German communities. Through learning how to praise, life was an exciting adventure.

Finding Strength in the Word

One of my true delights during that time was to sit on the second floor balcony and read the Psalms. The words, "I will lift up mine eyes unto the hills" became alive when I could raise my eyes from the pages of the Bible and look at the snow-crested Alps. No matter how I felt, the permanency of those mountains made me feel that this trial had been gone through and triumphed over before. If I would just hang on, I would see victory.

It was during one of those sessions that I asked God for a meek and quiet spirit. Since I have always had an opinion on almost any topic and have been most willing to share my "great insights" with anyone, I felt that asking for a meek and quiet mouth might be too much for this first time. However, I felt that I could handle a meek, quiet, and peaceful spirit.

Within days of that request, I became sick again. I knew what to expect this time and steeled myself for the severe abdominal cramps, the vomiting, the disorientation that comes with dehydration, and the inability to get out of bed. And come it did! Nothing seemed to help. I even told God I really did not think a meek and quiet spirit was worth all of this. I became so ill that Brother Scism (General Director of Foreign Missions) suggested we come home for an emergency medical leave.

I do not know when I have been so depressed as I was at that point. We had lived for our calling to Germany. We had made no other plans for our lives. This is what we were to do—and my weakness had caused failure. Because of me, my husband could not fulfill the call on his life. Because of this disease, my children would look at me with wide, haunted eyes. I hated my lot in life.

But those mornings on the balcony came back. "I will praise . . . I will praise . . . I will praise." David did not say, "I will understand," he only said, "I will praise." The psalmist did not even say, "I will like." He only said, "I will praise." It always seemed to come back to that one point. My time in Germany had taught me how to praise. But now came a time to learn how to practice praise in all circumstances.

The next months were difficult. We had nowhere to go. My father and his new wife graciously allowed us to stay with them and my husband entered a time of deep depression. Often he would not get out of bed and a voice inside my head said, "You caused this." My children would become very quiet and nonverbal. I knew they were struggling with circumstances of Crohn's and a voice inside my head would say, "This is your fault."

But there was a mountain. And often I would drive to a certain spot and, all alone, sit and look at Mount Hood. I would say, "I will look to the hills from whence cometh my strength. My strength cometh from the Lord who made heaven and earth. I will praise. I will praise." And I would receive strength and be able to face life again.

After nine months, an opening came in the Foreign

Missions Division at World Evangelism Center. We have been here since that time.

It has not been easy. I have had all but six feet of intestine removed. I have an ostomy and have to wear a bag to collect bodily waste because of a diseased rectal stump. I do not absorb nutrients from food well, so I have to have a permanent IV line in my chest for nightly feedings. This has repeatedly become infected and caused many blood infections.

One time the heart itself became infected, a condition called endocarditis. During that time, my temperature rose to almost 107 degrees. I do not really remember much of that time except being very cold. It was an inner cold that nothing but very sweet hot tea fed by the teaspoon would help.

The cause was found—my IV line had been put too close to the heart and a bacterial had built up on the damaged heart wall. Open-heart surgery was performed to remove the bacteria and repair the wall of the heart.

Many friends came to support my family as I went to surgery. I do not remember being afraid, but when I saw a pastoral friend walking down the corridor as I was being wheeled to surgery, I knew that everything would be all right.

No, it has not been easy. Russ Taft wrote a song about the anchor holding. One of the phrases says: "I've had vision. I've had dreams. I've even held them in my hand." I had only wanted two things in my life: to be a missionary to Germany and to be an elementary school teacher. I did both, but both slipped right through like they were only grains of sand.

Practical Lessons to Learn

This journey of praise has taught me many things, many spiritual but some practical. I close this chapter with some of those more practical lessons.

Know your body. You have a responsibility to understand how your body is reacting. Doctors are normally kind and knowledgeable, but your body has never read their medical books and may react totally different than the books say it will.

Go to your doctor with a pattern of symptoms. It is very helpful to go to your doctor's appointment with the pattern of symptoms. Keep a medical journal. Be able to say, "This seems to occur when" or "This happens just before . . ." The isolated symptoms may not help the doctor as much as the circumstances of each occurrence.

Keep a sense of humor. There are two things that the devil cannot imitate: a sense of humor and total praise. His imitations are so poor that they are easily spotted.

Find a doctor who fits your personality. Some people need a doctor who will not face an issue head on. Others need someone who will "tell it like it is." Neither is wrong, but you must find the one that fits your needs.

Do not be afraid to grieve. Any time a major part of your life is lost, whether a job, body part, or loved one, it is normal to go through the five stages of grief.

- ❄ *First is denial.* This isn't happening. If I am strong enough, this will go away. Nope, not me!

- ❄ *Next comes anger.* Anger? A child of God angry? Oh, yes! I was very angry with God. There were some that I saw pitying themselves because "they had to go to the mission field." I became very angry that I was not allowed to go.

- ❄ *The third stage is bargaining.* OK, this has happened, but God, if You will heal me, I will never again eat chocolate! Or I will pray for three hours a day and six hours on Sunday!

- ❄ *Depression normally follows.* An emptiness and

despondency often come when you realize that this is for real and possibly for life.

❧ *Finally comes acceptance.* For a child of God, peace comes with this stage. At this point, it becomes easy to raise your hands and say, "Lord, You do all things well. Life is not what I want it to be, but I am still going to praise You in the midst of a storm."

It is important to note that the person who is sick is not the only one who will go through these five stages. Anyone who is close to the person who is sick will go through the same stages. The entire family needs a support group who will help them.

Minister to Others

Look for someone to whom you can minister. I have been in the hospital so many times that I lost count. In fact, I began to call hospitalizations "medical evangelism." God always seemed to give me a roommate to whom He wanted me to talk.

Mrs. Washington and her daughter especially come to mind. The thirty-year-old daughter had had a stroke at a family reunion. I had experienced some problem and ended up in the room with them. We had Bible studies. We had services. We just had a good Pentecostal time! They were from Louisiana, and almost everyone who came to see me either knew the town they were from, the church they attended, or one of their relatives. I finally told them that I did have friends who were not from Louisiana.

Another time, Vida was my roommate. She was a Muslim, but she allowed me to pray with her. And pray I did! We were both crying when I finished. Vida looked at me as I was leaving and said, "I'm sorry you were sick, but you were sent here for me."

The Entire Family Needs Support

When a person is seriously or chronically ill, an entire family unit is sick. If the ill person is a woman, her first thought will probably be the care of her children. Friends can support her by taking her children and giving them a "normal" weekend. Let them talk. Let them play. Take them to McDonald's or on a picnic.

They can support the husband by helping with the laundry, cleaning the house, or providing a meal. Frozen meals which can be heated at the family's convenience are greatly appreciated.

There are situations in which no words can be of help. Those who visited me during the very hard times and simply held my hand while I cried were more comforting than those who tried to encourage me with words.

Yes, I have had some very hard times. Yet, I can truly say that I am blessed above all women. God has proven Himself so real and close that I could never doubt His love or His care. Above all, I have learned that in all situations I can praise.